10 TIMELESS PRINCIPLES

of Professional Success

Using the Life-Work Compass™ to Reach Your Potential

Steven R. Webber

Executive
Excellence
Publishing

© 2002 Steven R. Webber

For permission requests, contact the publisher at:

Executive Excellence Publishing
1366 East 1120 South
Provo, UT 84606
Phone: 1-801-375-4060
Toll Free: 1-800-304-9782
Fax: 1-801-377-5960
www.eep.com

For Executive Excellence books, magazines and other products, contact Executive Excellence directly. Call 1-800-304-9782, fax 1-801-377-5960, or visit our website at www.eep.com.

Printed in the United States

10 9 8 7 6 5 4 3 2 1

Library of Congress Cataloging-in-Publication Data

Webber Steven R.
   The 10 timeless principles of professional success : using the life-work compass to reach your potential / Steven R. Webber
        p. cm.

   ISBN 1-930771-22-3 (hardcover : alk. paper)
   HF5386 .W34 2002
   650.1 21
                        2001004696

Advance Praise for
10 Timeless Principles
of Professional Success

"It's a fun book that is a clear, concise, and thoughtful roadmap to both career and life success. Enjoy the ride!"
—Thressa Connor McMahon, vice president,
Welfare to Work Partnership/Chicago BizLink Operations

"This fast-moving book gives you a step-by-step process to get paid more and promoted faster, wherever you are in your career."
—Brian Tracy, author, *Success Is a Journey*

"Navigating toward a more purposeful, meaningful future has never been more important. This book provides some great tools to navigate to a more enriching future."
—Kevin Cashman, CEO, LeaderSource,
author, *Leadership from the Inside Out*

"Here we have practical ideas for professional growth as well as down-to-earth tools to manage today's challenges."
—Charles Garfield, Ph.D., author,
Second to None and *Peak Performers*

"Easy to read, highly practical, philosophically deep."
—Gifford Pinchot, co-author,
Intrapreneuring in Action

"The road to success is rarely easy or accidental. Steve Webber's book provides a powerful roadmap that will help you avoid the potholes while having a great time on the trip!"
—Chip R. Bell, author, *Customer Love*

Acknowledgments

Contrary to popular belief, the process of writing a book is not about proclaiming to the world what you know, but rather a lesson in self-discovery and personal growth. Throughout this literary journey, I have relied on friends and family for guidance and inspiration. As always, they have been a bedrock of support as well as a sounding board for my ideas. In addition to my inner circle of family and friends, I have met many other wonderful people who have also made a significant contribution to this book. I am grateful to all who have taught me more than I would have thought possible. I feel very fortunate for having had the experience of meeting and working with them.

To my wife, Amy, you have been the best partner in life any man could ever wish for. You have stood by my side through 24 years of marriage and have been a source of hope and inspiration more than you will ever know. Thank you for helping me keep my life balanced and in perspective. You are an amazing and insightful woman.

To my son, Brian, I am grateful for your kind, encouraging words that were always offered at just the right moment. It's been said that a man is measured by how big his heart is. If that's the case Brian, you are indeed a big man.

To my daughter, Missy, you are twice the writer I'll ever be. Your written word has a way of touching the human heart in a special way. I must have had God's ear the day I ordered you from life's catalog. You have exceeded my expectations in every way.

To my parents, Jack and Pat Webber, thank you for giving me the best childhood any kid could ask for. Dad, you have always been there as my safety net to catch me when I fell. You supported me in the big decisions in my life without criticism. Mom, you always made sure we never ran out of fun. You are an endless source of love. Thanks for all the sacrifices you made for me, my sister Carol Faber and her family, and my brother Mark Webber and his family.

Many thanks go to my account executive and office manager, Miriam Tavegia. Thanks for helping me meet all the last-minute deadlines I threw in front of you. I appreciate all the personal sacrifices you made to help our company grow. I couldn't have done it without you.

Thanks to the hundreds of clients I've had the opportunity to serve. Your faith in Management Training Resources is what has made our company grow. I have learned much by being privileged to know the inner workings of the many companies in which I have worked. The many lessons learned have been invaluable.

Thanks to Ken Shelton, the chairman and editor-in-chief at Executive Excellence, for giving me this wonderful opportunity to express myself through this book. Thank you for inviting me into your publishing family. Many thanks also go to Nathan Lyon, Courtney Hammond, and Mark Jessen, my editors. You have a special way of polishing the words that help make them shine. It is a joy to be associated with such professional people at Executive Excellence Publishing.

Other people who have contributed to this book include my sisters-in-law Jody Zenkel, Sue Falbo, and cousin Arlene Ross. I think they tried staying away from me while I was writing this book so as not to be badgered by my ongoing questions. Thanks for offering your comments and support.

Finally, I'd like to thank you—the reader. I wrote this book to help people like you. If you allow it, this book can be a source of knowledge and inspiration as you continue down your career path. My heart and soul went into writing it. I hope you enjoy it.

Contents

Preface

Over the past 20 years, I have worked with hundreds of companies and thousands of people in a variety of disciplines all over the world. Some of those disciplines have included the food industry, manufacturing, information technology, hospitality, government, the service industry, and health care. My work has led me behind the scenes to get a first-hand look at how people at all levels think and operate. I quickly learned that people, regardless of the industry they are in, complain about the same issues.

When I listened to the participants who attended my workshops, they would often say that the things that were frustrating to them were outside of their control. What's more, they felt it was the responsibility of others to make things right for them. I would often hear comments like, "It's not my fault," "There's nothing I can do about it," and "As soon as they give me what I need, then I can do my job." There was a general feeling of overall helplessness that contributed to their frustration. They all seemed to have something in common, however. Not only did they appear lost, but many of them were also unsure of what direction they should take in their career, and how to reach their destination.

I began to examine the issues more closely and discovered that most of the things people complained about were indeed things that they actually *did* have control over. But they didn't know how to create an improvement plan and then sustain momentum in the improvement process. Contrary to popular belief, I feel that there is much that people can do to improve their current situation, if they are willing to take personal ownership for their careers. Sadly, many people just sit around waiting for the "rescue bus" to appear so someone will save them. There is just one problem with that thinking: the rescue bus doesn't exist in real life!

In my workshops I keep track of what people say, how they feel about their jobs, and their opinions of people with whom they work and the customers they serve. As a result of many years of research, I have compiled a list of the top 10 mistakes people make that sabotage their careers.

1. Not being accountable for one's behavior.
2. Not having meaning and purpose in one's job.
3. No self-development plan for improvement.
4. Inability to communicate effectively with others.
5. Difficulty managing multiple priorities.
6. Little understanding of how to "play the game."
7. Resisting change.
8. Having a bad attitude.
9. Not having fun in one's job.
10. Not wanting to better serve the customer.

The purpose of this book is to identify clearly *what* the most common issues raised by workshop participants are, *why* they exist, *how* to eliminate them, and *when* to do so. My intention is to provide you with practical tools and techniques that will help you create a roadmap on how to navigate through these roadblocks that, sooner or later, appear in most people's lives and careers.

There are 10 chapters in this book. Each chapter focuses on one of the 10 common mistakes.

Chapters 1, 2, and 3 are designed around things that you can do by yourself, for yourself, without help from others. These chapters will help you develop a foundation of internal values for personal and professional success. They include:

1. Be Accountable.
2. Get Focused and Create Purpose.
3. Create a Self-Development Plan.

Chapters 4 and 5 are designed to enhance the skills that you will need to operate effectively within your organization. They include:

4. Communicate Effectively.
5. Manage Multiple Priorities.

Chapters 6, 7, and 8 are designed to enhance the knowledge that is necessary for you to become successful at the higher levels in your organization. They include:

6. Play the Team Game.
7. Be Open to Change.
8. Create a Positive Attitude.

Chapter 9 is designed to provide you with the balance that is necessary for your success, regardless of the situation. It is important to:

9. Be Playful.

Chapter 10, the culminating chapter, prepares you to apply your balanced values, skills, and knowledge to serve others. I believe that a good leader is a good servant. Therefore, it is important to:

10. Be Service Oriented.

At the end of each chapter, you will find a compass. The purpose of the compass is to summarize the main points of the chapter. However, instead of the north, south, east, and west points typically found on a compass, you will find they have been changed to what, why, how, and when. The comments summarized under each compass point can then be used to help you successfully navigate through your career—a life-work compass, if you will. There are five important comments under each compass point. When reading the life-work compass, start by reading all the #1 comments indicated around the compass. Then read all the #2 comments around the compass, and so on through #5. These comments flow easily from one point to another and guide you as you proceed on your chosen career path.

What you will *not* find in this book are theories, confusing steps to follow, buzzwords, jargon, cliches, or vague generalities. I think there is too much of that already out there. What you *will* find are timeless principles that are designed to help you become successful not only in your personal life but also in your professional career. If you're willing to open your mind to the possibilities and believe in yourself, you can reach success beyond your wildest imagination. Shall we begin the journey?

Steve Webber
Chicago, Illinois
February 2002

Be Accountable

Pointing Fingers and Placing Blame

Any good building contractor knows that the first step in building a house is a strong and solid foundation. If the foundation is weak, then the entire structure is in jeopardy of collapsing. Once the house is built, it is difficult to correct the problem. Repairs to the foundation can be made, but only at the expense of much time, labor, and money. Just as a strong foundation is essential to a well-built house, a strong set of values is necessary for your personal and professional growth.

In building a mature and successful life for yourself, you must be personally responsible and accountable for your behavior at all times. Pointing fingers and placing blame only hinder your progress.

Learning to accept responsibility and then to be accountable for one's behavior is the hallmark of a professional. These two values are not taught as well as they could be because we live in a society where accepting responsibility for one's behavior is rarely demonstrated and only occasionally practiced. When things go wrong, as they often do, a common tendency among many people is to point fingers and place blame on someone or something else. The "it's not my fault" mentality is immature, albeit pervasive. Rare is the person who is willing to become truly accountable and take ownership for his or her behavior.

Values drive behavior. If you want to know why people behave the way they do, all you have to do is examine their values. People behave in certain ways because of the values they hold. People who rise from mediocrity and become successful have, at some point, decided to take full responsibility for their lives and move in the direction of realizing their dreams. This is often called a turning point in a person's life and is the beginning of great things to come.

Placing blame on others for not fulfilling an obligation or meeting an expectation is immature behavior. It is often an attempt on the part of the person placing the blame to reduce personal responsibility and relieve pressure. When people place blame on someone or something else, they give up much of their personal power and enter the "victim" mode. This behavior is an attempt to remove the burden of responsibility from the individual and place it onto someone or something else. The immediate result is a reduction of pressure and tension. The long-term result, however, is a reduction of personal power and self-esteem. If you choose that direction, you will greatly limit your potential.

We see this finger-pointing behavior all around us. It is learned from a variety of sources—political parties blaming each other for the country's ills, adult children blaming their parents for psychological problems, management and unions blaming each other for the company's lack of productivity, and one culture blaming another for being unjust or unfair. We get a steady diet of this every day from people we come in contact with and from those we see and hear in the media.

It is rare today to find someone who is willing to accept responsibility for his or her behavior, regardless of the situation. To illustrate this, I have conducted an experiment in my training workshops over the last 20 years. When I ask people the question, "What are the major problems in your company today?" I have never heard anyone say, "The biggest problem in my company is me!" It's always the other guy. Have you ever heard a manager say, "Our department is responsible for the company losing money last month, and as the manager of the department, I feel it is only fair that I take some of the blame." Don't hold your breath—it'll never happen!

So, where does "it's not my fault" behavior come from? Psychologists tell us that human behavior is learned, especially during the impressionable years of childhood. Parents, relatives, teachers and friends, along with media personalities, help shape our values, beliefs and expectations. Good or bad, the child learns from others and then applies that learned behavior to daily situations—many times trying to see what he or she can get away with.

If people are taught to see themselves as powerless when they are children, there's a good chance that they will feel powerless as adults. When a boss or someone of authority challenges them later in life, they will tend to place blame on someone or something else for their shortcomings. A person with healthy self-esteem doesn't feel a need to constantly place blame. Being aware of the "it's not my fault" syndrome, and taking steps to eliminate it, will help you move toward reaching your potential.

Do you know people who make excuses anytime anything goes wrong? Regardless the situation, they have an excuse for not fulfilling an obligation. Examples include the people who claim they aren't good in math because they had a bad teacher, or the people who blame their parents for not giving them what they felt they deserved, or the person who doesn't have any money but blames the economy for not being able to get a job. These people have just entered the victim mode and carry these excuses in the form of a crutch to be used whenever it's needed. As long as that crutch is available, people will use it. Using a crutch to explain your shortcomings will diminish your personal power. If you are using a crutch, get rid of it immediately. The moment you decide to let go of that crutch is the moment you release your brakes and accelerate your momentum toward success.

A successful person is one who learns how to make the transition from blaming others and moves toward accepting responsibility for his or her personal life and professional career. Taking responsibility for your actions is the starting point for becoming successful. Having this value as the cornerstone of your belief system will help you build a solid foundation on which everything else in your future will be built. How do you demonstrate this? By making good choices in your life and then being responsible for those choices—no matter what happens!

Considering how difficult life can sometimes be, accepting responsibility at all times in your life is not always easy. In the space below, list an unpleasant situation that caused you to place blame on someone or something else. Consider the following example:

Situation: **Placed Blame on:**

Late for an important meeting   Road construction and traffic

_____   _____

_____   _____

In this example, this person blames their being late to a meeting with an important client on road construction and traffic. The fact is, the person knew, or should have known, that traffic was going to be bad and that there was road construction. Instead of taking responsibility and leaving a little earlier, this person chose to blame his tardiness on rush-hour traffic. The result was an unhappy customer. How easy it is to place blame on something or someone else.

In reviewing your own situation, was there anything you could have done to prevent the situation from happening in the first place? What is the current status of this situation? If the current situation is not what you expect, are you doing anything right now to fix it? If it happened again, would you respond differently? If so, how?

So far, we've been talking about people's reluctance to accept responsibility for negative situations. But what about taking credit for something positive? Here, there doesn't seem to be any shortage of volunteers. When things go well, many people come forward to grab credit, even if it is not deserved. Wanting to be recognized for a job well done is a very powerful motivator. This behavior is also pervasive in our society.

One of the best examples of correctly taking responsibility and being accountable for one's actions is the late Hall of Famer Walter Payton. Walter Payton is the NFL's all-time leader in running and combined net yards. He contributed 16,726 rushing yards with 100 touchdowns during his playing days with the Chicago Bears from 1975 to 1987. He holds the single game rushing record of 275 yards against central division rival, the Minnesota Vikings, and ran for over 100 yards in 77 games.

What is significant about all this? Not only was Walter an outstanding athlete, he was also a great role model. When he had a good game, the reporter interviewing him usually asked him about his accomplishments during the game. Walter would respond by praising and giving credit to his offensive front line, the coaches, and teammates. When he had a bad game, he would blame himself—how refreshing! Most people do just the opposite—how typical.

How does this example relate to the business world? Let's assume that you are a supervisor for a group of customer service people who take incoming calls from outside customers and then process their orders on the computer. It's now Tuesday morning after a three-day weekend, and already you've received several complaints from customers on how rudely they were treated by your people. When your boss finds out about the complaints, he approaches you, lets you know he is not pleased, and asks what's going on. Your response should be to look him right in the eye, taking full responsibility, and tell him that you will personally handle the situation immediately. Do not blame your people! Anything they do, or don't do, is a direct reflection on you as their supervisor.

On the other hand, let's say that your boss comes down to your office and tells you that she received a phone call from one of your biggest customers, letting her know how pleased they were with the service they received from one of your people. Your response should now be to defer the compliment back to your employee by saying, "Thanks, boss, Margaret is doing a great job. I'll be sure to tell her about the compliment." That is what Walter Payton used to do when he was playing.

I think our society is a little short on heroes today. By *hero*, I mean someone who not only is accomplished in one particular area of life but also uses that accomplishment to make significant contributions in other areas of life. In 1998, Walter Payton continued his many philanthropic works by creating the Walter Payton Foundation. Through his personal involvement and devotion to children's causes, he eased the suffering of many of our nation's neediest children.

Just before Walter's death in 1999, author Don Yaeger collaborated with Walter to write Walter's autobiography, *Never Die Easy: The Autobiography of Walter Payton.* "He had not just been a great football player," writes Yaeger, "he had been a role model in an age when role models were in short supply." On the back cover of the book Walter says, "If you ask me how I want to be remembered, it is as a winner. You know what a winner is? Winners are people who have given their best effort, who have tried the hardest they possibly can, who have utilized every ounce of energy and strength within them to accomplish something. It doesn't mean that they accomplished it or failed; it means that they've given it their best. These people are winners."

Walter Payton's legacy is monumental. The man they call Sweetness, for the way he ran, did not use his celebrity to gain preferential treatment to get an organ transplant. He is an outstanding example of how to live and die with grace and purpose.

Walter Payton died in 1999 of a liver ailment while waiting for an organ donor. As a result, his family has continued his legacy by creating Youth for Life, a nonprofit campaign committed to educating young adults about the life-giving gift of organ donation. And that is why Walter Payton is one of my heroes. He is a wonderful example of a person who accepted responsibility and was accountable for his behavior, both on and off the football field.

Fostering Accountability

Any good accountant can record debit and credit entries and chronologically post them to a ledger page. Creating a statement of transactions during a fiscal period can then be produced as a working document for future use. Similarly, being accountable for your personal behavior means that you can recall and explain every aspect of that behavior. Being able to recall specific events in your life and then learning from those experiences is a powerful way to identify and overcome any barriers that might be holding you back. That is why self-help gurus suggest recording events in personal journals.

Being accountable for your behavior means being aware of the internal power that you have and then using that power to help make good choices to achieve good results in your life. Like it or not, accepting or rejecting being accountable for your actions will have a profound effect on that situation and the consequences that follow. Being accountable for your behavior means that you take responsibility for 100 percent of your thoughts, feelings, emotions and behavior, regardless of the circumstances. This is the fundamental difference between people who are successful and people who would like to be successful.

In his book *Leadership from the Inside Out,* Kevin Cashman maintains that personal mastery begins when you take total responsibility for your life—not relying on someone else to identify who you are. Cashman writes, "No one else can validate your value. It is for you to give yourself. Leaders can effectively validate and support others only if they have validated themselves first." So, start by taking responsibility for your actions in order to create a solid foundation on which to build. This is the hallmark of all people who achieve professional success.

The only person responsible for your career success is you! The hard reality of life is that no one really cares about you the way you do. Relying on someone else to "save" you only leads to a life of frustration and cynicism. The beginning of a successful journey starts with a positive affirmation using three simple words: I am responsible! The next time you pass a mirror, look yourself in the eye and say, "I am responsible." Your behavior is the mirror with which you present your image to the world. Having done that, now go out and make something happen!

So far, I've been using the terms *responsibility* and *accountability* interchangeably. So what's the difference? Responsibility is one's duty to perform a given task or service to obtain a desired result. It usually comes from an outside influence, such as a parent, teacher, or boss. Accepting responsibility means trying to fulfill an obligation from another person.

Accountability, on the other hand, means behaving in a responsible manner in order to fulfill that obligation. It is an internal force that moves you in the direction of achieving the desired results for which you are responsible. Responsibility may be delegated to another person; however, accountability cannot be delegated. Accountability is like glue—it sticks to you no matter what. You are accountable for results or the lack of results. Keep in mind that no matter how much responsibility you delegate, the ultimate responsibility still lies with you.

One way to cultivate accountability, not only as an employee in the workplace but also as a parent in the home, is to behave always in a way that demonstrates responsibility by taking ownership for your own actions. This means doing what you say you will do. Remember, there are consequences to everything you say or don't say, as well as consequences to every action you take or don't take. When you blame others for your shortcomings, you give your personal power over to them. Why would you want to do that? Being responsible for your behavior is a broad-based value that can withstand much weight. Now, you're ready to build!

Us vs. Them Mentality

Another issue I have observed is the us vs. them mentality. This mindset often promotes a feeling of separateness, and if not managed properly, it can lead to potential conflict. Most people and groups like to differentiate themselves from others by declaring "I'm different," and therefore, somehow unique or "better than you." This can easily be seen by observing how people try to look different from other people in the clothes they wear, the music they listen to, the car they drive, the vacations they take, and the schools they attend.

While the philosophy of "different is better" may be useful when competing with other companies, it is not necessarily a healthy philosophy within an organization. Competing with other internal departments for the company's limited resources takes a great deal of time and energy—resources that could be employed better in serving the customer. What does it matter if operations receives the bulk of the budget if people in sales don't have the resources they need to sell the product? This is like fighting for deck chairs on the Titanic—everyone loses.

It is a good idea to steer clear of internal competition in your company when it involves "dirty tricks" or hurting other people to achieve a desired result. The short-term gain will usually hurt your career in the long run. When you are pressured to make a decision that affects others, ask yourself, "Will my behavior help serve the customer, my company, and myself?" If the answer is *no*, then walk away from that choice. If the answer is *yes*, then do everything in your power to make the situation or event happen. Your goal is to focus your time and energy on areas of common ground among the three factors of customer, company, and self. Consider the following diagram:

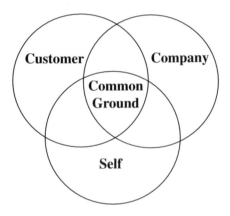

The philosophy of any company should center around the concept that "we are one." All departments working toward a common mission is necessary to help make a company grow and stay competitive. All employees in the company should know and understand the values of the organization and behave in such a way to support those values in their day-to-day activities. It is important to know where you fit in the overall picture and how your individual contribution impacts the organization as a whole.

Getting everyone pointed in the same direction is not easy. It's pretty hard to fight a battle when troops are charging in different directions. So, too, all employees in a company must coordinate their efforts and move in the same direction if desired results are to be achieved. Such corporate alignment is not easy to create. Consider the following diagram:

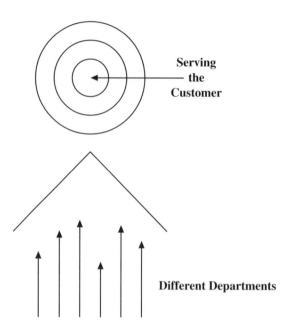

Different departments of a company, represented by the arrows, must be pointed in the same direction if the company is to function effectively. It is the responsibility of the company's leaders to identify the target and then energize employees to follow. Creating a vision and a mission statement is nice, but leaders must somehow articulate their vision into something that employees can understand, believe in, and embrace. Otherwise, the vision and mission statements are just nice sayings on the wall.

All employees must know their specific roles in the company. It's like being in a rowboat, knowing where to sit, and then rowing in the same direction to reach your destination. The leader identifies the destination; the employee helps him or her get there.

Do you know where your company is headed? What are your company's goals this year? How's your company doing? Is it having a good year? How are you contributing to its success? Are you rowing in the right direction?

You might also think of alignment in terms of aligning the tires on your car. If your car is out of alignment, it will tend to veer to the right or to the left. You must apply constant pressure on the steering wheel to keep the car moving straight. Your career success with your company is a lot like steering a car. You must know the direction your company is headed and then steer in that direction. If you need to schedule your "car" for an alignment, then do so quickly. Failure to do so will result in putting undue stress in your life and career and will move you away from your final destination of professional success.

Making Good Choices
Determine whether or not you agree with the following statements:

You are exactly where you are in life as a result of the choices you have made. You are the sum total of all the choices you have or have not made in your life. You are exactly where you are, at this point in your life, as a direct result of those choices. You are ultimately responsible for those choices. You are creating your life as you go, through the choices you make along the way. Good choices equal good results; poor choices equal poor results. Your choices are yours alone—no one else's. In the end, only you can determine if a given choice is best for you.

All choices have consequences—some good, some not so good. In the following space, reflect back on some recent choices that you have made in your life. Think about the consequences of those choices. Did you choose wisely?

Choice:	**Consequences:**
Eat fast food vs. healthy food	Weight gain, sluggish feeling
Not going to college	A life of average-paying jobs
_____	_____
_____	_____

I'm not saying that getting a college degree is absolutely essential to your success, although it helps. There are plenty of self-made people who don't have college degrees who are very successful. But if you wanted to go to college and did not, for whatever reason, that particular choice of not going has had some consequences in your life. Wouldn't it be nice to have a crystal ball to help us with our decisions?

How do you know if you're making a good choice? The answer to this question is simpler than it appears. If you have created some clearly defined, written and specific goals in your life, then making a decision that moves you in the direction of accomplishing your goals makes that choice a good one. If your choice does not move you in the direction of accomplishing your goals, then it's a poor choice. A good goal is a worthy goal, and a worthy goal is the one that creates meaning and purpose in your life.

Life really can be quite meaningful once you identify a destination and pursue it. People who have not yet decided on their destination are gambling on their future. That's a poor choice and a bad bet. People without goals are subject to the conditions and circumstances in their lives. In the next chapter, I'll show you how to write goals that are meaningful and fun.

It is important to make a distinction between solving a problem and making a decision. A problem is a situation that requires a solution. A problem exists when there is a gap between the current situation and what is desired.

A decision, on the other hand, is a choice between alternatives. Different scenarios include a single problem that requires a single decision, a single problem that requires 10 decisions, or multiple problems that require multiple decisions. Each scenario requires slightly different analysis. The nature of the decision will determine the amount of time and research that go into making it. Decisions regarding the direction you take in your personal life and professional career are important and should not be taken lightly. Remember, every decision you make or don't make has consequences.

In order to make good decisions, it is necessary to demonstrate good judgment. Judgment means weighing alternative courses of action before choosing. The ability to make a decision while demonstrating sound judgment is a skill that can be learned. It is important to understand that making decisions and using good judgment are two separate skills. Keep in mind that you can make many decisions but show poor judgment. Decisiveness deals with the quantity of your decision while judgment deals with the quality of your decision.

To help you better understand the difference between problem-solving and decision-making consider the following:

Problems	Decisions
My computer is obsolete.	Which computer should I buy?
We need to hire more employees.	Which person should we hire?
I have too much to do.	What should I do first?

Poor decisions are often made because not enough information is available. Some people can't seem to make a decision even when all the information is available to them. If you're having trouble determining when to make an important decision, consider making it when you have 60 percent or more of the information you need. Obviously, the more information you have available to you, the easier the decision. However, if you wait to make a decision when you have 100 percent of the information, it will probably be too late. Successful people don't gamble on their future, but they do take calculated risks. Other reasons that lead to poor decisions include:

- Diving in—failure to gather important information
- Not taking time to analyze the facts
- Letting your feelings or emotions get in the way
- Overusing your intuition
- Overconfidence in your judgment
- Winging it
- Being distracted by too many options
- Ignoring your core values
- Not learning from past mistakes
- Failure to properly follow up

To help you with upcoming decisions, consider the following six-step model for making decisions:

1) Clearly define your objectives. The clearer you are in identifying your target, the easier it will be to make good decisions.

2) Establish criteria. What is the scope or boundary of time or money in which your decision must fit?

3) Research and collect information. Use the Internet, library, or other people to get the information or advice you need.

4) Analyze alternatives. Determine the consequences of each decision.

5) Make the decision. Choose wisely.

6) Follow up. Monitor and follow up the consequences of any decision you make.

The future is purchased by the decisions you make in the present. Your happiness will largely be determined by the quality of those decisions. Failure to make a decision is a poor choice and a bad bet. Personal growth begins when you say it does. Starting today, decide to take total ownership for your personal life and professional career. Always be accountable for your behavior and 100 percent responsible for the decisions you make. Doing so will help you rise to levels you never dreamed possible and put you among the elite few who have decided to make a difference in this world.

Life-Work Compass

Principle One:
Be Accountable

What?

1. Take responsibility for yourself.
2. Hold on to your internal power.
3. Lose the us vs. them mentality.
4. Align yourself with your company's mission.
5. Make good choices.

When?

1. Starting today and at all times in the future.
2. Anytime you are challenged.
3. When you are confronted with a challenging situation.
4. When you are at work or in front of a customer.
5. When you have at least 60 percent of the information.

Why?

1. Because it's the starting point for professional success.
2. Because blaming others releases your internal power to them.
3. Because it promotes separateness and can lead to conflict.
4. To better serve your customers in a manner that the compa ny expects.
5. Because successful people don't procrastinate.

How?

1. By not pointing fingers and placing blame on others.
2. By being 100 percent accountable for your behavior.
3. By focusing your attention on the team rather than the individual.
4. By constantly moving in the direction of serving the customer.
5. By making choices that move you in the direction of accomplishing your goals.

Get Focused and Create Purpose

Creating Meaning and Purpose

The next step in your journey involves discovering what you want to accomplish in your life and career and then getting focused on doing it.

As a child, did you ever play with a magnifying glass? On a sunny day, if you positioned it just right, you could use it to collect the sun's random rays and concentrate them into a single beam of light. The sun is the source of all energy on planet earth as well as the rest of our solar system. Without it, all life would cease to exist. As powerful as the sun is, that beam of magnified light was even more powerful because it could be concentrated and directed at a single object. If the object you directed that beam of light toward was a piece of paper, you could easily start a fire.

Just as the magnifying glass magnifies the sun's rays into a single beam, successful people first create meaning and purpose in their lives and then focus their energy into accomplishing their purpose. Not having meaning and purpose in your life is like spraying your energy in all directions and trying to be all things to all people. Because your energy is finite, identifying what's really important to you is critical to your success.

Playwright George Bernard Shaw said, "If you take too long in deciding what to do with your life, you'll find you've done it." I have seen many people who I would describe as sleepwalking through life. These are people who haven't decided what they want to do with their lives. At some point in your life—and that point is different for each person—you must make a decision about who you want to be and then do everything in your power to become that person.

Some people try to avoid making the decision of who they want to be in life altogether, even when opportunity clearly presents itself. Some people are just plain clueless. What's more, they seem content with being clueless, which is okay, if that's the direction they choose—it's their choice. In his book *Napalm and Silly Putty*, George Carlin writes, "Most people don't know what they're doing, and a lot of them are really good at it." If you don't choose what you want to do with your life, life will choose for you. Then you have to decide if you like what life has picked out for you.

Psychiatrist Thomas Szasz said, "People often say that this or that person has not yet found himself. But the self is not something one finds, it is something one creates." I believe that all people were put on this earth for a purpose. Your job is to find out what that purpose is; sometimes, that's not an easy task. Remember that meaning and purpose in your life come from within. Follow your heart and create a life that is meaningful and purposeful to you.

People can have more than one purpose in life. When I was a youth, playing sports was very important to me. I looked forward to playing little league baseball. As I got older, college became important. After I graduated, a career was the most important thing. Then came getting married and raising a family. Today, my career is still important to me, but only after seeing that my wife and children are not only provided for, but have all of life's opportunities that will help them be successful and reach their full potential. Their happiness and fulfillment are very rewarding to me.

Avoid spraying your energy in a haphazard manner. Being all things to all people can be difficult and frustrating, if not impossible. You should relax and enjoy your life, but also have one or two things in your life that excite and energize your passion for life—something that is at the very core of your being.

Creating meaning and purpose in life is similar to ordering food from a menu. Your options include choices from categories such as beverages, appetizers, soups, salads, entrées, and desserts. For example, if you pick steak, do you want it prepared rare, medium-rare, medium, medium-well, or well done? You can fine-tune your choices to order a meal to satisfy the specific requirements that suit your taste. Just as you choose a meal from a menu, you can also choose how you want to spend your life. To help you get started, I have identified four categories that will help you create meaning and purpose in your life. They are personal, career, body, and spirit. There are probably other categories that could be included in our list, but for now, let's concentrate on just these four.

To help you examine the four areas, consider the following: In your personal life, you may wish to become a better listener and be more patient with your spouse, children, or other family members. Or, you may wish to volunteer some of your time at such places as school, boy and girl scouts, little league, church, or synagogue. In your career, you may want to go back to school and get that bachelor's or master's degree. For your body, you might consider starting an exercise routine and eating healthier food. In your spiritual life, you might consider taking long walks to relax and reflect on your life. To help you get started, consider the following questions:

If you could change one thing in each category, what would it be?

Your personal life: _____

Your career: _____

Your physical body: _____

Your spiritual self: _____

What is one thing that you would most like to accomplish in each one of these categories?

Your personal life: _____

Your career: _____

Your physical body: _____

Your spiritual self: _____

What do you feel is keeping you from achieving that one thing?

Your personal life: _____

Your career: _____

Your physical body: _____

Your spiritual self: _____

The answers to these questions will help you determine what is important to you. Those answers will also help guide you in a direction that is good for you. Keep in mind that you alone must identify what is good for you, so don't fall into the trap of letting other people choose for you, even though they may have good intentions and mean well. Your purpose in life is unique and special; you personally own it. What's your purpose?

Purpose is the reason you were born. Many people spend their entire life trying to figure out what their purpose in life is. Some never figure it out. So just what is the meaning of life? The answer to that question has perplexed human beings since the beginning of time. I would like to offer you an answer to that question. See if you agree with the following three things that may help you determine the meaning of your life:

- Everyone is born with a gift. Discover what your gift is.
- Develop that gift to its fullest potential.
- Then, share your gift with many others.

Sounds simple, doesn't it? The important things in life usually are simple. In fact, the things that are most important in your life are usually right there in front of you, if you only take the time to look. The questions you ask and the choices you make in life will help create your true identity. Author Erica Jong said, "Everyone has a talent; what is rare is the courage to follow the talent to the dark place where it leads." Make it your mission in life to discover your talent. Don't be afraid to go boldly forward.

How do you discover your purpose? On the Life-Work Compass, the "how" to discover your life and career purpose can be accomplished by asking yourself the following three questions: 1)What am I really good at?, 2) What do I enjoy doing?, and 3) Why do I enjoy doing it? The answers to these questions lead you toward finding meaning and purpose. In the following space, try to answer these three questions.

What am I good at? _____

_____

What do I enjoy doing? _____

_____

Why do I enjoy doing it?_____

_____

The answers to these questions will point you in the direction of creating your own personal path to success. Oliver Wendell Holmes said, "The great thing in this world is not so much where we are, but in what direction we are moving." Keep in mind that the path you choose in life belongs to you; it is the one that is right all the way down to your soul. Don't let other people persuade you to accept their version of what your path should be. All people are created for a purpose. Your life has meaning. Your job is to create the life you want—it's all up to you, and it's not too late to start.

The Power of Goal Setting

To create your future, you must first create your goals. *Successful people* set goals, *unsuccessful people* do not. Fewer than 5 percent of the American population commit their goals to paper. Most people think that if they just remember their goals in their head, that's good enough. This philosophy is for losers. If you're serious about reaching your potential, then writing down your goals is a must. The reason for writing your goals becomes clear because you have to think a little harder when transferring the thoughts from your head onto paper. Writing your goals also forces you to use more of your senses, such as sight and touch. When your goals are written, you can then read them repeatedly to ingrain them into your subconscious mind. Writing your goals fosters a sense of commitment.

If goals are so important to success, then why don't more people set them? There are many reasons why people don't set goals. Here are five common reasons:

- They simply don't know how.
- They haven't made a personal commitment.
- They feel it is a waste of time.
- They feel setting goals is for nerds.
- They fear success and/or failure.

Fear of success. We've all been afraid of failure; that's easy to comprehend. But what exactly does fear of success mean? To illustrate this, consider the person who would like to lose some weight. Everyone knows that eating a balanced diet along with regular exercise will help you live longer and feel better. However, many people think that they will have to give up something in order to achieve the things they want in life. They are reluctant to start because it may mean changing their current lifestyle—they fear success. What they don't understand is that a person who lacks the courage to start is already finished. Don't fear success. Make a decision to set some goals and get going.

Most people don't know how to set goals. In the past, few schools have spent any time teaching children how to write goals. Today, however, many schools are doing a much better job at teaching children the importance of setting goals and how to write them.

There are many models for goal setting on the market today. If you currently use a particular format that is comfortable for you, continue using it. Use what works for you. Basically, there are a few simple ingredients that all good goals should have. Let us start by examining a good personal goal statement:

Lose 10 pounds in two months.

First, goals should have a tangible number included in the goal statement. Notice that the number 10 identifies the amount of weight. Saying that you want to lose some weight does not identify how much weight, and it is not specific. You must have a tangible number included in your goal statement to help measure it. This number can be in the form of an actual number (lose 10 pounds); a dollar amount (make $80,000 per year); or a percentage (increase my savings account by 10 percent this year).

Second, the goal must have an end point. Two months identifies the end point for achieving the goal. This timeline represents the target deadline. By weighing yourself in two months, you can determine your success in trying to lose the desired weight.

Third, your goal should be attainable. Setting a goal to run a marathon next month is not very realistic. A good goal should have a 50-50 probability of success; that is still a stretch. Don't fall into the trap of setting your goals too high, and then getting frustrated because you don't achieve them. It is better to set your goals on the low side. After you achieve the goal, you can then set the next goal a little higher. It's important to have a pattern of success.

Start the goal statement with an action verb. An action verb is a word that describes action. Here are just a few examples of action verbs to use to begin your goal statement:

Accomplish	Coordinate	Improve	Reduce
Achieve	Create	Increase	Sell
Build	Design	Install	Start
Complete	Eliminate	Lose	Train
Conduct	Establish	Produce	Write

The written goal statement must be crisp and focused. The clearer the goal, the more likely that it will be accomplished.

Now that the basic steps for writing a goal have been identified, you are ready to write one for yourself. In the following space, practice writing both a work-related goal and a personal goal.

Work–related goal:_____

_____

Personal goal:_____

_____

Goals vs. Standards

What is the difference between a goal and a standard? The main difference is that a goal is finite—it has a beginning and an end—whereas a standard is ongoing. Sometimes, a person can set a goal to reach a standard. For example, your goal is lose 10 pounds; your standard is to keep the weight off. Once you reach the goal, obviously you should try to maintain it over time. Maintaining something at a desired level is called a standard. Think of setting goals and standards as an ongoing process of creating and maintaining.

Goals vs. Objectives

The words *goal* and *objective* are often used interchangeably, however, they are not the same. A goal describes *what* you are trying to accomplish, the objective describes *how* you will go about accomplishing it. In other words, objectives are activities that you perform to accomplish the goal.

Let's use the previous goal statement that states: Lose 10 pounds in two months. Losing weight is *what* you want to accomplish. *How* you do that could include: eating less, taking long walks, riding a bicycle, swimming, or doing aerobics. Any of these activities will help you lose weight. Your personal and career success should include both goals and objectives.

Aligning Your Goals

It's not enough just to write goals and work toward accomplishing them. Your goals must also be in alignment with your meaning and purpose in life. Your behavior must be consistent with the goals you set for yourself. To help you make wise choices, ask yourself: "If I do this thing, will it help move me closer to, or farther from my goal?" If the answer is *farther from*, then don't make that choice. For example, if you are trying to lose weight, then eating that jelly donut moves you farther away from your goal. Therefore, don't eat it.

To help you align your goals with your meaning and purpose in life, consider the following diagram:

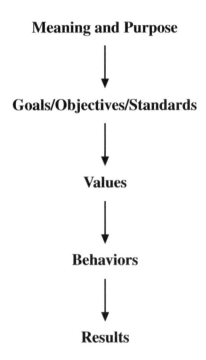

Meaning and Purpose

Goals/Objectives/Standards

Values

Behaviors

Results

To achieve the results you want, you need to create a plan to follow. The old saying, "Failing to plan is planning to fail," is true. A plan of action that is aligned with your personal goals and values is like a needle on a compass—it always points to your true north. If your personal plan is in alignment with your meaning and purpose, then it will always lead you in the right direction, regardless of the circumstances.

Goals are dreams with deadlines. Become a dreamer again, and don't be afraid to dream big dreams. Eleanor Roosevelt said, "The future belongs to those who believe in the beauty of their dreams." In his classic book *Think and Grow Rich*, Napoleon Hill concluded that successful people are all big dreamers. "If the mind can conceive, the body can achieve." Attach your goals to your dreams, and get ready to behold things that you never before thought were possible.

Choosing Your Values

Having strong values is the cornerstone of success. A "value" is something that you regard as important to you. I'm not referring to possessions, but to things that help build your character. People's behavior is often determined by their values. People with weak values might behave in ways that are not conducive to their own well-being and success. People with strong values increase their chances of reaching their goals.

To help you determine your values, consider the following list. Circle the values that are important to you. Add values that are not listed.

Assertive	Concerned	Caring	Honest
Forgiving	Involved	Respectful	Patient
Team-oriented	Understanding	Risk-taker	Loving
Persistent	Disciplined	Insightful	Daring
Outgoing	Responsible	Ambitious	Loyal
Goal-oriented	Motivated	Trustworthy	Bold
Supportive	Inclusive	Enthusiastic	Confident
Diplomatic	Determined	Sympathetic	Friendly
Humble	Calm	Gentle	Decisive
Conscientious	Poised	Observant	Responsive
Modest	Brave	Inspiring	Tactful
Strong-willed	Stimulating	Kind	Cheerful
Considerate	Firm	Logical	Joyful
Eager	Generous	Easy-going	Impartial
Lenient	Cooperative	Even-tempered	Vigorous
Neighborly	Helpful	Positive	Optimistic

_____   _____

_____   _____

_____   _____

Where do your values come from? Who was influential in your life? Who inspired you? Think of people who surrounded you in your childhood—parents, grandparents, teachers, sports personalities, friends, and clergy. Keep in mind that anyone can influence you in either a positive or negative way.

In an earlier example, I referred to one of my heroes, Walter Payton. To me, his behavior in life and in death demonstrated how a human being and a professional athlete should act.

I have also been blessed by having two of the most loving and caring parents a person could ask for. Both my mom and dad have influenced and supported me throughout my life. My wife and children have also had a profound impact on my life.

In the following space, list four people who have made a difference in your life, and state why.

1._____

2._____

3._____

4._____

Try to model your life after the people whom you admire. Pick the most positive traits from each person and create the ideal person. It's not possible to transform into this ideal person, but it's smart to move in that direction.

Regarding Ethics

How many times have you heard people say, "Do the right thing?" What does the word "right" mean—"right" according to whom? People disagree on what the right thing is. What one person thinks is right is often disputed by others. What is the difference between morals and ethics anyway? These words are bantered about today by people also claiming to be "right." Who's responsible for teaching our children morals and values? Is it the responsibility of parents, teachers, politicians, clergy, corporations, or a combination of all of the above? Ethical scandals are all around us.

One doesn't have to look very far to see the next scandal unfolding in the media. It's not easy trying to do the right thing these days.

Before we get too far, let's define the terms *moral* and *ethical*. *Moral* implies conformity to generally accepted standards of goodness. The word *moral* is often used to describe a person, as in "He's a moral person." We also hear people say, "She has a strong moral character." The term "generally accepted" refers to what is generally accepted in our society. This, too, is confusing because what once was not generally accepted now is. In 1963, the Beatles introduced America to a different hairstyle. Short hair, once the standard, soon became old-fashioned, especially with young people. Today, short hair seems to be back in fashion. Now, being bald is cool.

Ethics is generally used to describe how people behave or act, as in "He's an ethical doctor." Good companies have an obligation to provide their employees with clearly identified moral and ethical standards. Employees who work in that organization must adhere to the particular code of conduct in their relationships with all people with whom they come in contact. As an employee, you should promote your company's values and culture by behaving within the ethical guidelines established by your company. If you're not sure if a certain behavior is appropriate, you should ask. Not doing so can get you into hot water.

Ethical dilemmas occur when you find yourself in situations where making a clear-cut decision is difficult. You know you're having an ethical dilemma when you ask people for advice and their answer is, "It all depends." The challenge of doing the right thing now becomes even more difficult. Ask yourself, "What would I do?" to the following "it depends" situations:

- You learn that a co-worker is taking company office supplies home to give to their kids for a school project.
- You find out that a co-worker is using the company phone for personal long-distance calls.
- You learn that a co-worker is blatantly padding their expense account.

- You happen to know that the person the company is planning to hire has a drug problem.
- You know that a co-worker is having an affair with the boss.

How would you react to these situations? Do you speak up and tell someone, or do you find yourself saying, "It all depends?" Most people will base their decisions on whether it is right for them. People generally act in their own self-interest to suit their personal needs, then justify their decision as being "right." What is right for you may not be right for someone else. You will face many ethical dilemmas in your life; not all of them are bad. Much can be learned by facing ethical dilemmas. A smooth sea never made a skillful sailor.

Keep in mind that we're not talking about an occasional bending of the rules here. Be careful, however not to get too comfortable with the "just this once" syndrome. Rationalization can be dangerous. Over time, you may find yourself compromising your values to the point where it starts to negatively affect how you feel about yourself. Here are some questions to ask yourself the next time you are facing an ethical dilemma:

1) Am I doing anything illegal?
2) Am I doing anything I wouldn't want my spouse, children, or friends to know about?
3) Would I be embarrassed if this were made public?
4) Would I like someone doing this to me?
5) Will I compromise my values if I do this?

It's no crime to be imperfect. Learning from our mistakes is how we grow. The journey to discover who we are is a journey of personal growth that never ends. Along the way, however, you must be true to yourself and never compromise your values. When you concentrate on raising your ethical standards and then adhere to them throughout your life, you will be known as a trustworthy and dependable person. Build a positive reputation for having strong ethical standards and live by a moral code of conduct that others can aspire to.

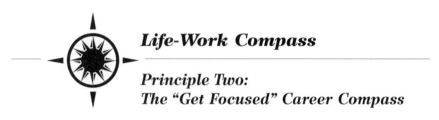

Life-Work Compass

Principle Two:
The "Get Focused" Career Compass

What?

1. Create meaning and purpose in your life.
2. Avoid spraying your energy haphazardly.
3. Focus on the four categories: personal, career, body, and spirit.
4. Set goals and objectives.
5. Develop strong values and ethical standards.

When?

1. This should be done right now; don't wait.
2. This should also be done now.
3. When you seem lost and don't know where to turn.
4. Do this when you have some personal quiet time.
5. Start from this day forward.

Why?

1. So you don't waste your life or your time.
2. Because you only have a finite amount of time.
3. To give you specific categories for personal and career development.
4. To provide you with clear targets.
5. To provide you with a code of conduct for life.

How?

1. By determining what you like and what you're good at.
2. By determining what is important to you.
3. Just answer the questions in each category.
4. By making sure they are specific, clear, and time-based.
5. By practicing the golden rule.

Create a Self-Development Plan

Your Shining Star

Would you ever consider starting a long journey to a distant place without a travel plan? Sounds foolish, doesn't it? Just as a travel plan is a key to a successful trip, a self-development plan is a key element in creating a successful life and career. Some people go to great lengths to plan a detailed itinerary for an upcoming trip but do not take the time to plan their life or their career. Upcoming vacations and trips can be very exciting and important, but aren't your life and career important too? If you don't have a life and career plan, you cannot know which direction to head. And, how will you know where you are going and how will you recognize when you get there?

In Lewis Carroll's *Alice's Adventure in Wonderland*, Alice, upon reaching the crossroads, looks up in a tree, sees the Cheshire Cat, and asks, "Would you tell me, please, which way I ought to go from here?" The cat responds by saying, "That depends a good deal on where you want to get to." "I don't much care where," said Alice. "Then it doesn't matter which way you go," said the Cat. "So long as I get somewhere," Alice said. "Oh, you're sure to do that," the Cat said, "if you only walk long enough."

We all know people who just seem to wander around in their lives, not really knowing where to go. There's movement all right, but movement away from what they don't want and don't like. A successful person is one who sets meaningful goals and then moves toward accomplishing them. That's a big difference.

So where do you start? No matter what stage of life you are in, a good place to start is by listing your strengths and areas for improvement. You don't need to list 100 items—just a few will suffice. What are you good at? What aspect of your life and career would you like to improve? List three things that you are good at and three things you would like to improve.

Strengths: **Areas for Improvement:**

_____   _____

_____   _____

_____   _____

Even when you know where you are going, the journey is still often filled with surprises. The life-work compass helps to point you in the right direction, and your self-development plan shows you the way. These two tools will help you become successful. It would be a big gamble to take the journey of life without these tools.

Five Focal Points

Your Shining Star is a model for your self-development plan. This model is simple and fun to complete. It consists of five focal points that, once developed, will help you reach your goals and become more successful. Your job is to create a customized action plan for each of the five categories.

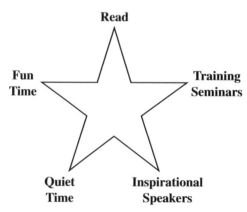

Let's examine each of the five focal points, as you will need to customize your own Shining Star according to your strengths and areas of improvement.

1. Read. If you're like most people, finding time to read is becoming more and more difficult. Many people today think that reading is not as important as it once was. Television and radio have helped replaced reading. TV and radio, however, do not go into enough detail, especially with today's "sound bite" programming. Reading, however, can provide you with as much information as you wish. You, not the media producer, are in control of your topic and how much time you spend digesting it.

Given the demands on your life, finding time to read can be very challenging. If you currently feel that you don't have the time to read, I suggest you start slowly by reading just 15 minutes per day. As a rule, the two best times for reading are the first thing in the morning and the last thing before you go to bed. Curling up with a good book at the end of a long day is a great way to unwind and relax.

The two best times of the day when your subconscious mind is most receptive to incoming information are the first thing in the morning just after you wake up and the last moments right before you go to sleep at night. Instead of starting your day reading negative things in the newspaper or watching dreadful news on television, try reading a book and feeding yourself with material that enriches the mind. How you start your day has a tremendous impact on your mindset for the rest of the day. Also, how you end your day just before you go to sleep can influence the soundness of your sleep. Try not watching local news just before you go to bed; it can be very depressing. Instead, read a good book or reflect on the things that went well for you that day.

What topics should you read about? The answer to that question is entirely up to you. However, there are four areas that you may want to consider: work-related, biographies, self-help, and fiction.

• *Work-related literature* will help you become more effective in your job and will propel you to the top. Some material may include a technical trade journal, a business book or magazine, a report on your competition, or a news feature on the latest technology. You want to be as current as possible with anything that is job-related. For example, if you are in the computer industry, read about the latest hardware or software trends. What is your competition doing? What are the features of your competitor's product? Why are people buying from them? What is your company doing to compete with them? What are the features and benefits of your products and services? Being knowledgeable about your company's products and services will help you become more of an asset to your organization and to your customers.

• *Biographies* illustrate how people achieve success in spite of setbacks and obstacles. What did they do that made them successful? What were the obstacles that they overcame? By reading about the lives of other people, you can learn what they did to become successful and perhaps do those same things in your own way. You might also avoid their mistakes. Select people whom you admire, read about them, learn, and emulate their success!

• *Self-help books* will help you improve your life in areas that relate to your purpose and goals. For example, if you would like to increase your reading and comprehension, find a book on speed-reading. If you would like to improve your memory, find a book on memory and recall. If you would like to improve your relationship with your spouse, find a book on relationships.

Samuel Butler wrote: "The oldest books are still only just out to those who have not read them." You can learn from any book, no matter when it was written. Knowledge is timeless; it knows no boundaries for those who are willing to learn.

• *Fictional stories* add depth and variety to life. Try not to limit yourself to non-fiction. Read some fiction as well, and note how the author develops the story and the characters. You can lose yourself in a story where the plot twists and turns, not knowing what will come next. It's a great way to relax and recreate.

If you want to improve as a reader, you might consider reading books that are a little beyond you. By stretching your mind, you force yourself to think. Unless you stretch and challenge your mind, your learning will be minimal. Therefore, be open to all topics, even ones that you do not like. Reading books will help you grow. You'll be amazed how much you can learn by reading. Not taking the time to read is foolish. Be smart—read!

For those who have little or no time to read, try listening to books on tape. Listening to a book on tape while commuting to and from work is an excellent way to digest a lot of material in a short time. It is also a great way to reduce stress while fighting traffic.

You can turn you car into a virtual learning center. If you spend two hours per day commuting to and from work, that represents 10 hours per week. A typical audio cassette book consists of three hours of listening. You could easily listen to two books per week, and over 100 audio books per year! Imagine the knowledge you could gain by listening to that many books, beyond the number of the books that you actually read!

2. Attend Training Seminars and Workshops. A good self-development plan contains seminars or training workshops offered in your field. Ideally, depending on the budget of your company and your time, you should try to attend four training programs per year, one per quarter. These programs can be technical, safety related, or relationship and behavioral in nature. It doesn't matter, as long as it is something that will help you in your job.

Most companies have money in their budgets for employees to attend seminars. You want to make sure you take advantage of that resource. If you don't, someone else will. Having your company pay for you to attend a seminar is a great way to learn. If you attend an outside seminar, you'll have a chance to meet other people from your industry and learn from them as well.

There are many sources for quality training. A good place to start is by looking at some of the trainers that your company has used in the past. Try to get some testimonials from previous participants as to the value of the seminar.

Another good source in finding training workshops is the Internet. Look up key words that relate to the topic of your interest. For example, you might type in the word "leadership" and see what comes up. Don't be afraid to call the company to interview the trainer over the phone. Personally, I love it when someone calls me or sends me an e-mail to inquire about our training programs. If I don't offer what they want, I actually refer them to some of my competitors. Since I know my competitors pretty well, I can guide the caller to someone who can meet their specific needs.

A quality training company has both good content and the right person to deliver it. I believe that the most important element in training is the right person to facilitate the material. The speaker must make a connection with the audience. Establishing rapport with the participants is an essential ingredient to any quality training program. If the presenter can connect with the audience, learning will automatically take place. A good trainer can make the dullest of topics come alive. Don't be afraid to interview the presenter and ask for references before the training session begins. After all, it's your time and money.

3. Inspirational Speakers. Pick people whom you admire and find out when and where they will speak. To speak with an author, you can call the publisher of the book and ask how to contact the person. Often, an address or phone number is listed at the back of the book. You can also check your local newspaper for an announcement of who will be coming to town. The Internet is also a good resource. Well-known speakers usually have their own Web sites. Also, they may be represented by a publicist or speakers bureau that you can contact.

Many universities publish a list of speakers who are scheduled to appear at the university throughout the year. If there is a college or university close to you, you may wish to inquire about how to purchase tickets. You can also visit the university's Web site to find out more information as well. Some universities have a speaker's forum where they schedule a new speaker each month. This is a great way to hear from someone who is world famous. Try to pick people from different walks of life. Some of my favorite speakers have been Madeleine Albright, Colin Powell, and Oprah Winfrey. Try to attend sessions presented by both men and women.

4. Quiet Time. It's becoming more difficult to create quiet time these days. Many people have trouble doing this because they are so busy answering phone calls or responding to their beepers and faxes. We are taught to be fast-paced, result-oriented, multi-tasking people: "Make it happen," "get it done," "be the best," "go for it." How about doing nothing and just being? What's so wrong with that? Sometimes a person just needs to turn the world off for a time and just do nothing—just be. After all, we are human *beings*, not human doers.

I'm a morning person, and so I try to take a few minutes early in the morning for quiet time. In the summer, I go out on my screened-in porch and just listen to the sounds of nature and watch the sun come up. Many creative ideas pop into my head during this quiet time. I've done this many times to get ideas for this book. It's my favorite time of the day. It's also a great way to recharge my batteries for the upcoming events of the day.

I use this time to plan my day or to strategize how I'll approach a difficult situation that's facing me. I try to avoid jumping out of bed and rushing into my day. When I do this, I find that I'm usually running behind all day long. I never seem to get caught up, no matter how much I try. That's very stressful. Taking a few minutes in the morning for myself is a great way to start the day.

If you're an evening person, try to take some time at the end of each day to reflect on the day's events. What went well? What could have been better? Did you do anything that made a difference in someone else's life? Did you miss any opportunities that presented themselves to you?

Watching the sunset is a perfect way to end the day. When was the last time you watched the sun set? Mother Nature gives us this spectacular show every night. It doesn't cost anything, and you don't need tickets to get a good seat. Sharing a sunset with loved ones is a great way to connect with them and just be.

5. Fun Time. I subscribe to the notion that "All work and no play makes Jack a dull boy." A person's life should be balanced with work as well as play. I see many people who pile up their vacation time at work and then have trouble taking it. This is not good!

You've earned your vacation, and you deserve to take it whenever you want. Balance is one key to having a successful life. Schedule your vacations and take them. Try not to let the events of the day interfere with your plans. Something will often come up at work at the last minute. Let other people deal with it—you're on vacation! Remember, no business person ever said on his deathbed, "I wish I'd spent more time at the office."

Don't be afraid to try new things and go to new places while on vacation. Or just stay home and relax. Try not to take a vacation day here and there. You will likely spend the day working on a project. Consequently, you come back to work more exhausted than when you left. Try to schedule two weeks off at a time. I know this may be a luxury in your business; however, taking two weeks off will help you to really relax. Before you leave for vacation, avoid telling your boss where you are going. If people know where you are and how to reach you, chances are they will. If you're going with your family, don't you and they deserve a break from all the business as usual?

Besides taking a vacation, what are some fun, relaxing activities that you enjoy doing? Consider the following list of ways to relax:

Listening to music	Taking a walk
Playing a sport	Having a hobby
Playing cards	Taking a hot bath
Visiting a friend	Playing with children
Going to the movies	Watching television
Sipping a drink	Lying in the sun
Reading a good book	Exercising
Practicing Yoga	Taking a snooze
Gardening	Looking at a photo album
Having your hair done	Getting a massage
Enjoying a sauna	Visiting an art gallery
Surfing the Internet	Going dancing
Having dinner at a restaurant	Going on a picnic
Doing a crossword puzzle	Playing a board game

In the following space, add some of your own ideas on how you might relax:

_____   _____

_____   _____

_____   _____

Your Action Plan

Creating a self-development plan is like planning your trip through life. It is an important element in reaching your goals. Your plan will help you identify the direction to take in pursuing the things that are important to you in your life. On your Shining Star, you can substitute any of my categories and insert your own. You might add such things as health, education, spirituality, and family. Any category will do, as long as the activities in that category help move you in the desired direction toward personal growth.

Take a moment now to list five categories in which you'd like to focus and create your Shining Star.

Persistence—The Key to Your Success

The critical factor that separates successful people from unsuccessful people is persistence. It is the key ingredient to your success. Just as bread will not rise without yeast, success cannot happen without persistence. A plan is the first part to reaching your full potential; taking action is the second; being persistent is the third. Consider the following formula for success:

$$Success = Plan + Action + Persistence$$

Many people have positive attitudes and have set clear goals but still fall short of their aspirations. Successful people have the ability to get up after they've been knocked down—again and again. The ability to bounce back after a disappointment or failure separates the winners from the wannabes.

Think of your life as a rubber ball. When a rubber ball is dropped on concrete, it bounces back. A glass ball, on the other hand, breaks. A failure is someone who thinks in terms of the glass ball. Keep in mind that we all fail at certain things in our lives—it's how we learn. However, if you give up after a failure, you indeed have failed. The trick is to bounce back! Confucius said, "Our greatest glory is not in never falling, but in rising every time we fall."

Here are some quotes that inspire me to persist:

"Nothing in the world can take the place of persistence. Talent will not; nothing is more common than unsuccessful men with talent. Genius will not; unrewarded genius is almost a proverb. Education will not; the world is full of educated derelicts. Persistence and determination alone are omnipotent."

—Calvin Coolidge

"Never, never, never give up."

—Winston Churchill

"I know of no such unquestionable badge and mark of a sovereign mind as that of tenacity of purpose."

—Ralph Waldo Emerson

"Always bear in mind that your own resolution to succeed is more important than any other one thing."
—Abraham Lincoln

Physical Fitness

You already know that developing your intellect is important to your success, but what about your body? Think of your body as the vehicle in which you live. Just as a car takes you where you want to go, your body is the part of you that takes you where your mind and spirit want to go. Maintaining your car regularly will make it last longer. A new car is a major investment. Maintaining it gives you a better return on that investment.

Your body, like your car, is an investment too. Fuel your body for the performance you desire. Smoking, drinking, and overeating are not healthy habits. They lead to breakdowns. If you combine those habits with a sedentary lifestyle, you have sealed your fate.

I do not advocate trying to change your entire lifestyle all at once with the latest exercise gimmick or diet. Buying and doing those things only makes someone else rich. I do believe, however, in finding something that is right for you. You know your body better than anyone else. Try not to let other people tell you what is right for you; only you can know what is right for you. Taking steps toward improving your body through diet and exercise is moving in the right direction. The trick is to go slow and make incremental improvements over time. This approach to fitness is hard to follow since we live in an "instant" society and are programmed for "now!"

A good place to start is by looking at a chart that describes the ideal weight for people based on their gender, height, and age. Use this as a guideline to help you set a goal for your ideal weight. You don't have to look like the models in the magazines. However, you do want to try to look and feel your best. Maintaining your body is just as important as maintaining your car. Use the goal-setting model listed in Chapter 2 to help you write your goal for improving your physical fitness. Start slow and easy, but start today!

When you choose an exercise routine, pick something that you consider relatively fun. Most of the exercise equipment on the market today is very expensive to buy. Health clubs, too, can be expensive if you join for one year or more and then stop going to the club after the first month. Not only are you still not exercising, but you now feel guilty for wasting money. So what can you do?

First, don't beat yourself up for missing a scheduled exercise routine. You don't need to take any guilt trips when it comes to improving your body. I always like to tell people that I exercise every day—except for the days I don't. You're not out to prove anything to anyone except yourself. Do whatever feels right for you, regardless of what the so-called "experts" say. You are your own referee when it comes to your body. The key, however, is being consistent. Start slow and gradually build to the next level when you are ready. Keep in mind that some exercise is better than no exercise.

I try to adhere to a certain exercise program as much as possible. I share my program with you only because it might give you some ideas for creating your own routine. It combines lifting weights as well as doing aerobic exercise and eating a sensible diet.

Always warm up before you begin any exercise routine by stretching your muscles. Warm muscles burn fat; cold muscles burn sugar.

In his book *Prime, The Complete Guide to Being Fit, Looking Great, Feeling Great,* author Bob Paris talks about the importance of stretching for people over 40. He states, "In fact, stretching is so important to people over 40 that if I were forced to make a single choice between weights, cardio, and proper stretching, I would have to choose stretching." Most injuries occur because of the lack of stretching or improper stretching before a workout. Regardless of age, take the time to stretch your muscles before working out.

In week one, exercise two days a week concentrating on your upper body by lifting weights for the arms, shoulders, and chest. Each workout is just 45 minutes long. Don't overdo it. Spend two days doing aerobic exercise on a stationary bike or treadmill. Each workout is 20 minutes long. You should try to break a sweat, however. Exercising four days a week is good enough, and they don't have to be consecutive days.

In week two, concentrate on your lower body by lifting weights for the legs and stomach. Again, each workout is just 45 minutes long. You can increase the amount of weight you use when you are ready to increase it. Don't strain yourself, but try to push yourself on the last few repetitions. Spend two days a week doing aerobic exercises as well.

For those of you who are really into weight lifting, exercise and diet, I suggest reading the book *Body for Life* by Bill Phillips. He is an expert in his field and will tell you everything you want to know about becoming fit.

You should have a goal for your ideal weight. Keep track of how much you weigh using a weekly chart. Simply record your weight each week until you get to the weight you desire. Your clothes will start to fit better and look better on you after the first few weeks. You'll feel better too—so don't give up.

In terms of eating, I like dietary drinks. They're loaded with vitamins and are easy to drink in the car on my way to a meeting with a client. You may have to experiment with different brands until you find one that appeals to your taste. Eat a sensible lunch and dinner. On Sundays just relax, eat what you want, and start again on Monday. When picking an exercise routine, consider your age, fitness level, and what feels right for you.

As we get older, we tend to become inactive. Inactivity is the road to a host of health problems. Being active and eating nutritional foods can put you on a path to wellness. Herein lies the challenge. We're a nation that values convenience and instant gratification rather than nourishment and health. Fast-food restaurants are everywhere, but that does not mean you choose burgers and fries every time you visit one. Good choices of nutritious meals can still be made at those restaurants.

Life-Work Compass

Principle Three:
Self-Development Plan

What
1. Create a self-development plan.
2. Read books.
3. Attend training seminars.
4. Create quiet time for yourself.
5. Eat right and exercise.

When
1. Today.
2. Read for 15 minutes in the morning or evening each day.
3. Attend three to four training sessions per year.
4. First thing in the morning or last thing at night.
5. From this day forward.

Why
1. Because a person without one is gambling on the future.
2. To enrich your mind and become an expert in your field.
3. To learn from subject-matter experts.
4. To help balance yourself out from life's busy pace.
5. To live longer and feel better.

How
1. Use your "Shining Star" format.
2. Read books or listen to books on tape.
3. Sign up for classes offered by your company.
4. Plan your day to free up 15 minutes each day.
5. Customize an exercise program that fits your lifestyle.

Communicate Effectively

Understanding the Problem

Lack of communication is the number one complaint by today's employees. Constant changes in the workplace cause continually changing expectations on the part of both internal bosses and external customers. Unfortunately, this is normal and a regular part of doing business in an ever-changing world.

In this chapter I provide you with some techniques for clarifying these expectations and communicating effectively with anyone. Becoming a good communicator can greatly enhance your success.

My experience as a consultant and trainer suggests that at the root of the problems in the workplace today is a breakdown in communication. In fact, I would say that 90 percent of the problems in today's workplace are communication-related. After all, aren't most problems in our society communication-related? What do teenagers say when they complain about their parents? "My parents just don't understand me. They're so out of it." When a husband and wife are going through a divorce, the man might say, "My wife just doesn't understand me." And the woman might say, "My husband doesn't listen to me." Both sides complain about the other not being attentive to personal needs.

These communication problems can be broken down into the following categories:

- Misunderstanding
- Miscommunication
- Inaccurate information

- Misinterpretation
- Unclear expectations or no expectations
- Unclear goals, objectives, and standards
- Lack of coordination between other departments and shifts
- Not being "kept in the loop"
- Failure to update people with the latest information
- Failure to communicate changes
- Information overload
- Not caring
- Not taking the time to listen

Time is an element of communication. We often hear people lament, "There aren't enough hours in the day. We're just too busy to listen to each other." To become a better communicator, you must take the time to listen and care about what people are saying. If you take the time to listen, your relationship with your loved-ones and with the people at work will greatly improve.

One of the best examples of miscommunication during wartime occured in a battle that took place during the Crimean War in 1854 called "The Charge of the Light Brigade," made famous by Alfred Lord Tennyson's poem by the same name. The British Lord Raglan ordered Lord Lucan to "advance rapidly to the front." Lord Lucan misinterpreted the message and ordered his troops, consisting of 600 men, into a well-fortified Russian position. The Russians proceeded to slaughter over 400 of the original 600 men. The attack was suicidal and should not have taken place. What Lord Raglan meant was for Lord Lucan to advance his troops to the front, whereby they could reinforce other troops for an assault at a later time. Lord Lucan's misinterpretation of the message cost his men their lives.

Communication problems can have dire consequences. However, with all the tools, technologies, and gadgets available today—faxes, e-mail, the Internet, cell phones, and laptop computers—you would think that there would be fewer communication-related problems. Not so. On the contrary, there seems to be more problems today than ever before. Why? One reason is that people are still using the technology, and people make mistakes. For this reason, effectiveness on the job requires you to be a good communicator and to know how to use the various communication tools available to you.

Information Overload

One of the biggest problems in communicating today is dealing with the relentless stream of information made available to us from television, radio, infomercials, newspapers, billboards, magazines, books, the Internet, company intranets, e-mails, faxes, and laptop computers. Before you can digest today's data, tomorrow's incoming information is already on its way.

The abundance of available information presents a major challenge in trying to connect with other people. Your job is to cut through all the non-essential junk and select the information that helps you meet your objective. This is not easy. You only have so much time available to you. Try to be very selective about what you read and how much time you spend watching television. Try to spend more time with people who are important in your life. That is time well spent.

Before you communicate with someone else, you must decide what method of communication to use: phone, fax, letter, e-mail, or personal meeting. Your decision on what communication medium and method to use depends on your intent and to whom you are sending the message. Your goal is to try to make it as easy as possible for the other person to receive the information you are sending. If you're not sure, ask them what method they prefer.

Information overload is a common problem in your effort to become a better communicator. When communicating with others, consider three things:

- Whom you are communicating with
- The time frame for communicating the information
- What medium and method of communication to use.

Elements of Communication

When looking at a map, you need to understand all the symbols, lines, and colors. Otherwise, how do you know what you are looking at, and what it all means? The process of communication also has elements that are important to understand. Breaking down the communication process and looking at each element will help you better understand where potential problems might come from. The six basic elements of communication include:

- *Sender*—the person sending the message
- *Receiver*—the person receiving the message
- *Message*—information being sent
- *Encoding*—how the sender frames the message
- *Decoding*—how the receiver interprets the information
- *Barriers*—anything that gets in the way

Sender (encodes) ⟶ **Receiver (decodes)**

The sender encodes the message from his perspective while the receiver decodes (interprets) the message based on her understanding of what is being sent. However, since there are no two people exactly alike, this presents a potential barrier because people process information based on their own interpretation, perspective, values, and views. The encoding and decoding elements have the greatest potential for causing communication problems.

Think of the communication process as two people playing catch with a ball. The first person encodes the information (throws the ball) to the receiver who decodes the information (catches the ball). The receiver then throws the ball back to the sender, and the process repeats itself. A good game of catch is where both players are throwing the ball in a rhythm to each other. A bad game is where one or both players throw the ball in a way that makes catching it difficult for the other person. Both players must understand how the game is played and be a willing participant if they are to have fun.

When you engage in dialogue with another person, both of you are encoding and decoding the message simultaneously. Encoding the message means putting the message in a format that is consistent with your personality and values. This means that you are simply talking in your normal tone of voice from your own perspective.

Decoding, on the other hand, is more difficult because it requires you to interpret the message that is being sent. You try to decipher and comprehend the information in a way that makes sense to you. The challenge becomes one of understanding the message the way the sender intended. There is room for error every time two people talk.

The Values Filter

The potential for misunderstanding is great. This is because people filter incoming information through a set of personal values. This "values filter" is a set of personal values, beliefs, perceptions, expectations, and attitudes toward life. This filter is mostly developed in us by the age of 10 years old.

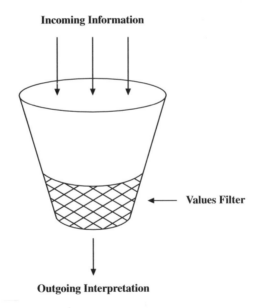

For example, I was born in 1954 in Michigan City, Indiana. So, by 1964, my values were largely formed as a result of my experience with my family, teachers, and friends. Natural events like civil unrest, the Vietnam war, and popular music influenced my life as well as how my parents raised me and the traditions we celebrated. Each of those events and experiences had an impact on how I interpret the events of the world today.

What were some of the things that influenced you? Consider but do not limit yourself to the following influences:

Clothes	School	Favorite music
Favorite food	Religion	Brother/sister
Cars/trucks	Summer jobs	Boyfriend/girlfriend
Holidays	Vacations	Toys
Bicycles	Sports	Games
Sports heroes	Swimming	Travel
Aunts/uncles	Chores	Neighbors
Your bedroom	Traditions	Birthdays
Favorite class	Best friend	Favorite teacher
Family pet	Mom/dad	TV shows
Cartoons	Movies	Hairstyles

Did any of these topics conjure up childhood memories? In the following space, list the things that made an impact in your life by age 10:

_____   _____

_____   _____

_____   _____

Consider that each person you come in contact with has a different values filter that is unique to them. You can now see why it is sometimes so difficult to connect with other people, especially when they come from different cultures. Every incoming piece of data passes through that person's personal values filter. Based on the mind's interpretation of that data, a judgment of either good or bad, yes or no, right or wrong will follow. One's interpretation of the information is what causes problems in the communication process between sender and receiver. It is, by far, the biggest barrier to communication.

To illustrate this point, think of something that recently happened in your job. Perhaps the boss said that there will be new computers installed at your workstation, or that the office will be rearranged to accommodate the new employees, or the company has announced a merger with another company. Do you have an opinion on these things? Of course you do. However, without knowing many of the details, you probably already made a decision about the upcoming change—either good, bad, or wait and see. Those opinions form your expectations about the future, and they are based on your interpretation of the information available to you. If any information is missing, your mind fills in the gaps based on your life's experiences or perceptions.

When you receive incoming information, your goal is to try to suspend judgment by unclogging your filter to let information flow out of the funnel just as freely as it came in. Doing this will help you become a better listener. This is hard for people who only hear what they want to hear. These people's filters are clogged—there's nothing coming out! A person with a clogged filter is someone with a fixed and rigid position who is unwilling to budge, even when the facts are presented effectively. Do you know someone like this? Aren't they annoying? Do you like being around them?

I think that it is important not to jump to conclusions. Try to give people the benefit of the doubt. An old Indian proverb suggests that you not judge another person until you've "walked a mile in his moccasins." I think that's good advice. Remember, a mind is like a parachute: it only works when it's open. If your goal is to enhance rapport with other people, then it's important that you try to remain neutral when listening to them. As soon as you start passing judgment on what they said, you begin to ruin the rapport. Hold your tongue and just listen!

The Three Vs of Communication

The three basic methods of communication are:

- Verbal
- Vocal
- Visual

Verbal means the words that you use when you speak. *Vocal* means the tone of voice you use when you write or speak. *Visual* means the body language that you use when you speak. Can you guess which one of these has the most impact in the communication process? Here are the numbers:

- Verbal   7%
- Vocal   38%
- Visual   55%

Verbal, the words you use, make up only 7 percent of your message. Vocal, your tone of voice, makes up 38 percent of your message. Visual, your body language, makes up 55 percent of the message you communicate to others! That's why a picture really is worth a thousand words. Consider the road signs when you drive the highways. Aren't they mostly visual? Isn't that a good thing?

The biggest impact you have when communicating with other people is your body language—the visual aspect. Over half of what you try to convey is interpreted by the other person based on how you look when you are talking. Consider the following ways you can communicate to another person without saying a word:

Smiling	Nodding your head
Frowning	Scowling
Rolling your eyes	Sitting forward in your chair
Behaving restlessly	Drumming your fingers
Having eye contact	Not having eye contact
Squinting your eyes	Shrugging your shoulders
Bouncing your leg	Looking surprised
Looking bewildered	Shaking your head
Sighing heavily	Tapping your foot
Folding your arms	Puffing your cheeks
Having hair combed/or not	Wearing clean, pressed clothes
Having your shoes shined	Wearing colors that match
Standing up straight	Crouching over

All of these things play a crucial role in how the receiver receives the message you are sending. Remember, the other person is interpreting your body signals through their personal values filter. Are you sending the message you intend to send?

It is important that you use your body in a way that is consistent with the words you use. If you don't, you will be sending a mixed message. This is where you say one thing but your body says another. It's like telling someone to get excited about something when your body has a negative look about it.

Many managers complain that their employees are reluctant to visit their office, even though they have invited them. Perhaps the manager's body language is saying, "Don't even think about it," even if the words appear to be inviting. Your body must be in sync, or alignment, with the words you use. Holding your hands and arms open when inviting a person into the office is more believable. That message is in alignment with the words and is more believable.

When you communicate, your body language represents over half of your message. People typically remember how you look rather than what you say. When your body reflects the same message as your spoken words and your tone of voice, you are sending your message in a very powerful and meaningful way.

Establishing Rapport With Others

When you meet someone for the first time, you probably form an opinion of that person within two seconds. That opinion will either be positive, neutral, or negative. Even before the person speaks, you form a first impression, usually based on visual appearance. That's why it's so important to always look your best.

When you meet someone new, within two seconds or less mentally ask yourself two questions: 1) "Do I like you?" and 2) "Can I trust you?" The answers to these two questions will determine how you feel about that person. Keep in mind that biases and prejudices come into play here, whether justified or not. How you feel is how you feel, and it may have nothing to do with the facts. Your first impression can be very subjective. The other person's body language, clothes, hair, and general appearance are visual clues on how that person wants you to judge him or her. Only after talking with this person, do you begin to form a more objective impression of the person.

Having good rapport with others means that you are in harmony with them. It means that you share something in common and feel comfortable being around them. You might even look forward to being with them because they are fun to be around and they make you feel good. The best way to establish rapport with another person is to be a good listener. Taking the time to listen to someone else says that you value the other person and consider what he or she says to be important. You are willing to give him or her something that is very valuable to you—your time. In her book *Listening—The Forgotten Skill*, Madelyn Burley-Allen says, "Of all the time we spend communicating, by far the greatest is spent in listening." Listening to someone else says, "I care about you." What a great way to increase rapport with others.

Three Keys to Becoming a Better Listener

Being a good listener is the most important skill you can develop to become successful in your career. Like it or not, it's important that you get along with others, even the people whom you don't like. If you have trouble doing that, you will have a difficult time gaining access to higher levels in your organization. If the influential people in your company don't like you, for whatever reason, you're not going anywhere. You will become plateaued in your career. To help avoid this, become a good listener. Everyone likes a good listener.

In *The 7 Habits of Highly Effective People*, Stephen Covey says that we should: "Seek first to understand, then to be understood." We tend to like people who listen to us. For example, think of people whom you like at work. Do they listen to you? Chances are, one reason you like them is because they are good listeners. Now, think of people you don't like at work. Chances are, they don't listen to you.

The skill of listening is crucial to enhancing your relationship with another person. Empathic listening is the best way to establish rapport with others, and it's not all that difficult! The failure to listen is the single biggest reason why people don't get along with each other. The ability to listen to others is the single most important human relations skill in the world! So how can you become a better listener? Here are three things you can do to become a better listener:

- Acknowledge the *feelings* and *emotions* of others as you suspend judgment of them.
- Stay in the *other person's world.*
- *Ask questions* to enhance the dialogue.

Let's take a look at each one of these three points to make sure you understand their significance. Remember, the whole reason you are using these techniques is to establish rapport with other people. The nice thing about these three things is that they can be used with anyone, whether you like them or not.

1. Acknowledging the feelings and emotions of others as you suspend judgment shows you value them. As soon as you criticize them, you begin to dismantle whatever rapport you may have had. I am not suggesting that you are never to disagree with another person, but I am suggesting that you hold your tongue and let other people talk without interrupting them. People's feelings are their truths.

One's feelings = One's truths

When a child comes crying to its mother about something that just happened with someone else, the mother typically will say to the child, "Oh honey, you shouldn't feel that way." This is a loving attempt by the mother to protect her child from the hurt he or she is experiencing. However, just because the mother says to the child, "Don't feel that way," doesn't mean the child will change his or her feelings. Think about it. When you're angry at someone or something and you hear the comment, "You should not feel that way," does that instantly change the way you feel? Of course not.

How people feel and what they believe to be true are truths to them. When we criticize other people, we are challenging their beliefs. Challenging people's beliefs is a good way to reduce rapport significantly. When you acknowledge the emotions of others, you enhance your rapport with them.

When acknowledging the emotions of others, consider responding with the following neutral comments:

"okay"	"I see"	"uh huh"
"really?"	"then what?"	"that's interesting"
"how?"	"allright"	"you're kidding"

These comments are neutral in nature and serve as a catalyst to continue the conversation. This encourages the other person to continue talking about whatever it is they are talking about.

2. Staying in the other person's world means not stealing the conversation when the other person takes a breath. For example, if a person you are talking with starts telling you about his vacation to Disney World last month, don't interrupt him and start telling him about your experience when you were there. Your focus should be on his vacation, not yours. Staying in the other person's world will help promote the dialogue between you.

3. Asking questions is a great way to show your interest in the other person. A question also leads the conversation in the direction of the questioner. The person who asks the questions controls the conversation. Do you agree? By directing the question back to the person to whom you are talking, you will generate further dialogue. It says, "You talk; I listen." Here are some questions that focus on the other person:

- A probing question asks for more detail: *"Can you give me an example?"*
- A reflective question rephrases the other person's comment: *"So if I understand you correctly, you feel that we should..."*
- An open-ended question requires further discussion: *"Why do you feel that way?"* or *"What's your opinion on...?"*
- A closed-ended question requires a one-word answer and should be used sparingly if you want to continue the discussion: *"Do you like chocolate cake?"*
- A leading question leads the person in the direction you wish to take them: *"You do like scary movies, don't you?"*

When you start to tell people something or criticize them on what they've done, you will quickly reduce any rapport that you may have established. Few people like other people who criticize them. Stay away from such comments as "I would never pay that much." This comment says, "I talk; you listen." Who wants to be around a know-it-all anyway? People who have opinions on everything are annoying to be around, especially when they try to convince you that their opinions are always right. Don't let that be you.

Think of someone with whom you would like to enhance your relationship. Use the techniques outlined in this chapter and practice on him or her. Even if you mess up the techniques, what do you have to lose?

Here are several suggestions for improving your listening skills:

• *Find areas of common interest.* One of the quickest ways to find areas of common interest is by asking questions. Be curious about what the other person is saying. Use follow-up questions to promote dialogue. For example, if a person is talking about her vacation, ask her to elaborate. You might find that you both share a common interest about what you enjoy doing on vacation.

• *Hold your rebuttal.* Don't let your emotions get the best of you. If the topic of conversation is something that is near and dear to your heart, wait for the proper time to share your thoughts on the subject. Try to comprehend what the speaker is saying before you interrupt him or her with your views on the matter.

• *Keep an open mind.* Try to suspend judgment when someone is talking about something with which you disagree. Religion and politics are good subjects to avoid, especially at work. No one is "wrong" in their mind. They just have a different point of view than you. Try to keep your mind open.

• *Analyze body language.* Be sensitive to other people's body language. Try to listen between the lines for hidden meanings. If you are sensing that the other person is uncomfortable with the topic, quickly change to something else.

• *Take the initiative.* Don't be afraid to start a conversation. Start with chitchat on general topics like the weather, traffic, or last night's game. If you talk about something in the news or on television, it's a good bet that someone has read the same story or has seen the same show.

• *Tell a story.* One of the best ways people learn is through the telling of stories. Personal stories have a way of engaging your audience and making a point. If you are talking to more than one person, remember to use eye contact with everyone. Don't exclude people by not looking at them when telling a story.

The written word is another important part of communicating with others. Paying careful attention to grammar, mechanics, and content can go a long way to enhancing your image at work. One of the most common methods of written communication today is e-mail. Here are some tips for effective e-mail:

• *Tightly organize.* The average computer screen is usually limited to 24 or fewer lines. Say what you have to say in one screen. Don't make your reader scroll through several screens trying to decipher your message.

• *Hit your reader fast and hard.* Make your point in the first sentence. This is what is called the topic sentence. It sets up the rest of the paragraph. All content in a paragraph should support the topic sentence. Avoid wordy sentences.

• *Use direct language.* Use direct rather than indirect language. Indirect language does not call the reader to action, as in: "Would you like to sit down?" Direct language makes a statement, as in "Please sit down."

• *Avoid vague words and phrases.* Avoid vague words like "bigger, faster, better." Bigger, faster and better than what? Avoid vague phrases like, "we need to tighten our belts," or "we need to work smarter, not harder." Does anyone really know what these phrases mean?

• *Limit slang, jargon, and acronyms.* Consider who will be reading your message. If the person to whom you are sending your message is not from your company, avoid using terms that only internal employees know.

• *Use proper grammar.* E-mail is an informal way to communicate. However, that does not mean you can forget the proper use of grammar. It is rude to your reader not to properly capitalize, punctuate, and organize content.

• *Send the message to whom it was intended.* Avoid spraying your message to everyone. This is the lazy way to communicate. Copy only those people who need to receive the information. If you're not sure, ask before sending.

• *Don't copy the sender's message in your reply.* Try to create a new message unless you need to refer to something specific in the original message that was sent to you. Deciphering everyone else's comments is a time-waster.

• *Don't use company computers for personal use.* Messages can often be retrieved even after they're deleted. Your message can be intercepted and read by anyone who knows how to manipulate the system. Always be professional when using e-mail. The written word leaves a lasting impression.

Life-Work Compass

Principle Four:
Communicate Effectively

What
1. Improve your relationship with a challenging person.
2. Unclog your "values filter."
3. Use positive body language when interacting with others.
4. Ask questions to understand the speaker.
5. Use proper e-mail etiquette.

When
1. The next time you interact with them.
2. When you interact with a challenging person.
3. Anytime you personally communicate with others.
4. When you need to be clear about what is being said.
5. Anytime you send an e-mail message.

Why
1. To reduce tension between the two of you.
2. To enhance your relationship with them.
3. To encourage dialogue.
4. To reduce any misunderstanding.
5. To save your reader time and enhance your image.

How
1. By asking follow-up and reflective questions.
2. By suspending judgment.
3. By keeping your body in an open position.
4. By asking the speaker to clarify or elaborate.
5. By using short, direct, grammatically correct language.

Manage Multiple Priorities

Do You Have a Choice?

Have you ever been on a road trip when all of a sudden a detour pops up? If you must detour onto unfamiliar roads, the side trip can be very annoying. Life, too, is filled with detours. Mother Nature has a way of picking interesting times to mess with us. In making your life's journey, you will be required to make millions of decisions. Choosing between them is not always easy.

Every choice has a consequence, even the ones we don't make. We often hear the comment, "I had no choice. I had to." That's not always true. Often people get themselves into difficult situations by making poor choices. If they had made better choices at an earlier time, then they would never feel they had "no choice." Successful people plan and prepare themselves for upcoming events, and then make timely choices to create the situation they desire. They make conscious choices to create their own future.

Managing your time is all about choices. People often say, "I don't have time." Usually they would have time—they just made poor choices. Then many people start to make lame excuses and start pointing fingers and placing blame on someone or something else. Successful people are accountable for their behavior.

Let's get one thing clear right from the start: No one can "manage" time. There are 24 hours in a day—no more, no less—and it is all available to you, every second of it. It really comes down to the way you choose to spend the time available to you. From this idea we get the term "self-management," because what you are doing is managing the time available to you.

What are you doing with your time? If you do not choose wisely, you will waste your time. It's all a matter of choice. How you choose to spend your time determines how you choose to spend your life. Good choices create a good life. Poor choices result in a poor life. What determines the value of your choices? Whether they move you in the direction of accomplishing your goals. It's that simple! Controlling your personal time means choosing to do the things that you know you should do, when you know you should do them—no excuses!

Focus on Things Over Which You Have Control

The first step in self-management is to focus on the things over which you have control. There's no sense wasting your time by trying to control things outside of your control, like the weather or someone else's behavior. Your time and energy is valuable and should therefore be spent wisely. Take a look at the following two lists. On the left are things you can control, and on the right are things that you cannot control.

Things you can control	*Things you can't control*
Procrastination	Requests by co-workers
Ability to say "yes" or "no"	Telephone/cell phone ringing
Cluttered work area	Equipment failures
Disorganization	Interruptions
Lack of personal goals	Unplanned meetings
Doing everything yourself	Outside activities
Failure to listen	Company "red tape"
Blaming others	Mistakes of others
Socializing	Actions of others

The first step in self-management is to identify your top time wasters and develop an action plan to eliminate those things over which you have control. Most people seem to have trouble with three time wasters: procrastination, the inability to say "no," and a disorganized work area. Let's discuss each of these.

1. Procrastination is something that almost everyone does that gets them into trouble from time to time. Procrastination simply means intentionally putting something off, for whatever reason, justified or not. It is, by far, the single biggest waster of time. Mark Twain quipped, "Never put off until tomorrow what you can do the day after tomorrow." This is poor advice when it comes to procrastination. Putting something off is like looking at a compass when you're lost, identifying the direction you wish to travel, and then waiting. It doesn't make sense.

Psychologists tell us that the leading cause of procrastination is fear—the fear of failure, fear of looking bad, or fear of ridicule by others. Fear of failure very often leads to a feeling of guilt. Not only have you chosen to put something off, but you now feel guilty for not doing what you know you should be doing. There's a lot of psychological "baggage" associated with procrastination.

In the following space, list something that you are procrastinating right now. It might be something as simple as cleaning out a closet or as difficult as starting a challenging project at work.

_____

_____

_____

One technique that you can use to help overcome procrastination is called "chunking." It simply means breaking the task down into smaller bites that are more manageable. This is especially helpful if the project cannot be finished in one day. Writing this book, for example, took several months to complete. I tried to set aside some time every day to work on it. Some of those chunks of time were spent researching material, interviewing people, or actually sitting at the computer and writing.

Look at the tasks on your procrastination list and pick one that is causing you concern. In the following space, try to break down that task into three separate chunks or activities:

Set a start and finish time for each item, and get started. Taking small steps will help you feel good about yourself. Before you know it, the task is half done. Don't forget to reward yourself for completing tasks. Rewarding yourself can make the thing you are procrastinating more enjoyable.

2. The inability to say "no" is another huge time waster. Many people, in an attempt to be nice, say "yes" to other people's requests, which usually means dropping whatever they are doing to accommodate the other person. Why should you inherit someone else's crises due to their inability to plan properly? When you say "yes" to someone else's interruption, you are reinforcing unacceptable behavior. In essence, you are saying "please feel free to interrupt me anytime you wish, and I'll drop everything to accommodate your request."

When you drop whatever you are doing to accommodate someone else, in an attempt to be nice, you diminish your personal respect. This is not good. Many people indicate that they would like to be shown more respect by others. One way to command respect is to say "no" to someone else's requests in a nice way. Please feel free, however, to drop whatever you are doing to help others. Just keep in mind that there are consequences to that decision. So, how do you say "no" politely?

One technique that works when saying "no" to someone else is to offer an alternative. This will help soften the "no." For example, if someone at work asks you if you have a minute, you might say, "I can't talk to you right now because I'm preparing for a meeting. But I will call you after my meeting, and we can talk then." The other person may be somewhat annoyed by your response; however, you will create respect for your time and reduce an annoying time waster. It is important, however, that you follow up with this person. If you don't, that person might perceive that you really don't care. By following up, you show that the person can trust you and that you care about the request.

3. A disorganized work area also contributes to waste. Think about the area where you work. What does it look like? If it is messy and disorganized, you are creating a difficult environment in which to work. Many people feel overwhelmed when they first enter their work area in the morning. That's because their work area is cluttered with stuff piled everywhere. When you enter your work area, you want to feel good about being there. Part of that good feeling comes from your work area being organized.

If your work area is cluttered, consider the "one-year rule." Throw out or file anything that you have not physically touched during the past year. If you have not touched an item in one year, chances are that you will never touch it again, let alone need it. Throw it out or file it away out of sight. Just having those things removed from your work area can help you start to feel good about being there.

Remove all magazines that may be stacked on your desk. Or, copy an article you wish to read and file it. Then when you have some time, you can always retrieve that article and read it. Better yet, delegate to someone else and have him or her read the article and give you a brief report on it. You may wish to cancel your sub-scription to any magazine that doesn't offer much value.

Clear everything off your desk except the project or task you are currently working on. Distractions occur when your eyes glance at other stuff on your desk. You think, "Oh yeah, I need to do some-thing with that today, too." You need to create single-minded focus on the task at hand. If you prioritize properly, then the thing that you are working on is the most important and urgent task to do any-way. Multi-tasking is a good skill to have; however, it is not good when you face a deadline on an important project.

If you relate to these three time wasters, what can you do to reduce their negative impact on your day? First, you need an action plan. Look at the list of things you can control. Pick just one time waster you wish to work on and list it at the top of the page. Then respond to the following statements:

My Action Plan:

Time waster I can control: _____

This time waster is probably caused by: _____

By not taking action on this time waster, I may lose:

_____

By doing something about this time waster, I will gain:_____

My plan of action on this time waster is to: _____

_____

Prioritizing Your Activities

There are many models on the market today on how to prioritize activities. Basically, there are only two criteria to consider to help you prioritize your daily activities: urgency and importance. Urgency is determined by the word "deadline." If the deadline for a task is staring you in the face, then the task is very urgent. If the deadline is off in the horizon, then the task is not very urgent.

Importance can be determined by the word "value." If you do the task, what value will it bring to you and others? If the value is low, then perhaps you should choose another, more important task. When choosing how to spend your time, consider both urgency and importance.

Start by creating a daily "to do" list. In the following space, list the things that are waiting for you when you return to your office or work area.

_____

_____

_____

Now, prioritize these items in order of what's *urgent* and what's *important* using the following diagram:

	High	Low
	Level B Priority	Level A Priority
IMPORTANCE	Trash	Delegate
	Low URGENCY High	

If something is neither urgent nor important (lower-left quadrant), then trash the task. Do not spend time on it. For example, you might trash the task of opening "junk" mail.

If something is urgent but not important (lower-right quadrant), perhaps this task could be delegated to someone else. By delegating the task, you are perhaps helping the person develop and grow. Any task can be delegated to anyone at any time. It's just a matter of trusting that the person can accomplish the task.

A "B" priority (upper-left quadrant), is something that is important but not yet urgent. This is where your choices become very critical in managing your time. Do you delegate the task, trash it, or do nothing and let it become an "A" priority? Your choices here will determine how you spend your time in the future.

An "A" priority (upper-right quadrant), is something that is both urgent and important and should be done right away. If this task cannot be done in one day, then you should "chunk" the item by breaking it down into smaller, more manageable pieces. For example, if your "A" priority is a week-long project, you might spend one hour each day on it. By the end of the week, you will have accomplished it.

Prioritizing your daily tasks should be a simple and enjoyable thing to do. Spending a lot of time prioritizing your tasks is a time waster itself. I recommend that you prioritize your tasks for the next day at the end of the current day while every-thing is still fresh on your mind. You can now go home and spend the evening with your family and friends, unfettered by your unfinished work. Tomorrow is another day. Your work will still be there when you go back.

When scheduling your priorities, take into account your "high energy time." Are you a morning, afternoon, or evening person? If you are a morning person, you might consider scheduling your "A" priority for the morning hours when your energy is high. Putting off an "A" priority for the evening will mean struggling to accomplish an important task with low energy.

The high-energy time for each person is unique to that person. So, try to work on important projects when you have high personal energy. Without knowing it, you can sometimes work against your own energy reserves. The likely result will often be less than your best effort. Life will not always allow you to plan activities according to your high-energy time. Being aware of your energy shifts, however, can help you do outstanding work consistently.

Prime-time hours occur in the morning between 9 a.m. and 11 a.m. and in the afternoon between 1 p.m. and 3 p.m. These are the hours of the day when most people are working. These are generally high activity times. Try to work on major projects during NON prime-time hours. Why? Prime-time hours are when you will receive most of your interruptions during the day—the boss sticking her head in your office, co-workers interrupting you, phone calls from customers, phone calls from other departments, etc. If you are trying to do important work during these hours, you will be interrupted.

If you're a "morning person," you might consider coming in an hour early in the morning to work on an important project during your high-energy time when there is no one in the office. If your company allows flex-time, perhaps you can work something out with your boss to leave a little early at the end of the day to offset the early hours.

When you go out to lunch, try leaving early to beat the crowd. You can be back at work when everyone else is out to lunch. This can be some additional quiet time to work on projects.

If you're an "evening person," try starting work a little later in the morning and staying a little later in the evening. You can avoid rush-hour traffic by leaving later and have some quiet-time at your desk or work-station after everyone else has gone for the day. Try working during off-peak, non prime-time hours. This strategy may not work every day, but this strategy comes in very handy when you're under tight deadlines.

If you have more than one "A" priority on your "to do" list, how do you know which "A" to do first? Numbering your priorities in order will help you focus on what "A" to work on first: A1, A2, A3. There are two ways to help you determine your A1 priority: 1) If you could do only one thing on your list, what task would you do? 2) If you did nothing on your list, what item would cause you the most pain because you didn't do it? By answering these two questions, you can easily determine your A1 priority. Now go back to your "to do" list and indicate your A1, A2, and A3 priorities. Also, try to schedule your A1 priority during your high-energy time.

Delegation

To be a good manager of people, you must know how and to whom to delegate. When you delegate activities to others, consider two criteria: responsibility and authority.

Responsibility simply means fulfilling an obligation. *Authority*, on the other hand, means having the power to influence and make decisions when carrying out a task. Effective delegation means delegating both responsibility and authority. Delegating responsibility without authority says to the people to whom you delegate, "I don't trust you." If they have to come to you for approval on all delegated tasks, then what's the purpose of delegating to them in the first place? It's like telling someone to bake a cake but not letting them go into the kitchen. This is a great way to lower morale. Consider the following diagram:

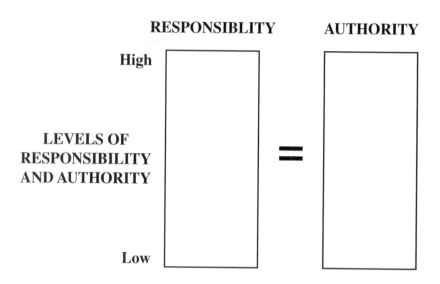

Trust is a central issue in delegation. When delegating an assignment, you must delegate the authority to match the responsibility. Make sure you take the time to discuss with people where their authority lies during the project or task; they must be crystal clear about their level of authority during each assignment. If they don't know where this boundary is, they will usually find out the hard way—by being "zapped" by the manager.

How many times have you been "zapped" because you didn't know your level of authority on a particular project or task? Did you find out the hard way? This is where the manager says, "Who gave you the authority to do that?" or "Why didn't you do what you were expected to do?" If this has ever happened to you, it is probably because your level of authority was not clearly established with your boss at the time of the assignment.

To reduce the potential for "zapping," simply ask your boss, "What authority do I have as I carry out this assignment?" "If this comes up, should I call and talk to the customer?" "If that comes up, should I talk to the VP, or should I call you?" "If you aren't available, who should I call in your absence?" Not knowing the answers to these questions can have dire consequences and can ultimately hurt your career.

When delegating work, consider the following guidelines:

- Delegate the entire project—don't save the good parts for yourself and delegate the bad parts to the employee.
- Make sure you delegate authority to match the responsibility.
- Don't overload one willing employee and disregard other capable people.
- Don't promise rewards for doing normal delegated work.
- Be willing to give up some of your favorite work to others.
- Refrain from "hovering" over employees when they are working.
- Be available for questions from the employee.
- Follow up with employees from time to time—check back with them.
- Support their decisions during the delegated task.
- Congratulate them on a job well done.

If you have employees reporting to you, you have the responsibility to develop them to the best of your ability. Delegation is one of the most powerful ways to develop your employees. This means you must collaborate with the employee to create a developmental action plan.

Make Meetings Count

Another big complaint I hear in organizations is, "There are too many meetings!" It never fails that when you need to ask someone something, you find out they are in a meeting. It seems they are always in a meeting. What are they meeting about, and what is so important that they can't take a few minutes and answer your questions?

"When it comes to meetings," said Michael LeBoeuf, Professor Emeritus of Management at the University of New Orleans, "most of us behave as though we had never heard that time is money." Effective meetings can provide us with information that is both timely and beneficial. Ineffective meetings can be a major source of frustration, especially meetings called for no apparent purpose. Whether you are attending the meeting or are the one who called it, you need to observe some definite do's and don'ts.

• First, you must have an agenda. Not having one is not an option. Anyone who calls a meeting and does not provide attendees with an agenda is foolish. There must be a definite purpose for the meeting. What are you trying to accomplish? What do you want the attendees to do as a result of the meeting? Who needs to be there and who doesn't? When should you hold the meeting and where? These are all good questions to ask before every meeting.

• Distribute the agenda to all attendees before the meeting. This can be done with a simple e-mail. The message should say, "Please come prepared to discuss . . ." This helps people to prepare for the meeting and cuts down on wasted time. If there is no time to send the agenda beforehand, you can either distribute it at the beginning of the meeting or simply write the agenda on a flipchart or whiteboard and discuss it at the start of the meeting to create expectations. This agenda should be posted throughout the meeting for all to see.

Here is a simple agenda format for a one-hour meeting on customer complaints:

Today's Agenda

8:00 to 8:05	Why we're here—purpose of today's meeting
8:05 to 8:15	What our customers are saying about us
8:15 to 8:30	Why these complaints are occurring
8:30 to 8:55	What we can do to eliminate these complaints
8:55 to 9:00	Summary, action items, assignments

• Keep people focused on achieving the purpose of the meeting. The agenda not only establishes expectations but also serves as a tool to refer back to during the meeting if people start to go off on a tangent. If that happens, you can simply refer them back to the agenda and defer the discussion to a later meeting if necessary. If you called the meeting in the first place, you must do this; otherwise, you will not meet your objectives. Moreover, other people will look at you as an inefficient meeting manager.

• Not all meetings need to occur during work hours; however, if you do hold them during work hours, try to hold them during non prime-time hours. Again, prime-time hours are between 9 a.m. and 11 a.m. and from 1 p.m. to 3 p.m. These are the hours when most people are working at their desks or workstations. During these hours, you need to keep people focused on getting their work done. If you're constantly in meetings during these prime-time hours, you are frustrating employees and customers who are trying to get in touch with you.

• Controlling group dynamics among participants during meetings is another important element of conducting an effective meeting. If you are in charge of the meeting, you must not only focus on covering agenda items, but make sure that all participants in the meeting are focused and contributing to results. Much money is wasted in unproductive meetings. If you have 10 people present for a one-hour meeting and these people make an average of $30,000 per year, that equates to roughly $300 per meeting-hour. Time spent in meetings is costly. Here are the common causes of ineffective meetings:

Before	During	After
Lack of an agenda	Socializing	No minutes
Wrong people	Allowing interruptions	No follow-up
Wrong time	Wandering from agenda	No action
Wrong place	Indecision	No accountability
Inadequate notice	Failure to start/end on time	No measurement
Not starting on time	Failure to summarize	No rewards

Another thing to consider is when to hold a meeting and when not to hold a meeting. There are alternatives to holding meetings.

When to hold a meeting:
- To clarify an issue
- To inform people of an important issue
- To share problems or concerns
- To brainstorm ideas on how to approach a problem
- To satisfy people who want a meeting
- To continue a team-building initiative

When NOT to hold a meeting:
- Confidential issues need to be discussed
- Inadequate preparation time or poor data
- Personal issues (promotions, transfers, discipline)
- Trivial subject
- Too much anger or hostility regarding the topic

Alternatives to holding a meeting:
- Make the decision yourself
- Send a letter or e-mail
- Send a representative
- Telephone conference call

Each type of meeting should have specific objectives and focus on getting results. Is the purpose of the meeting to inform, discuss, decide something, plan, coordinate, get feedback, train employees, or celebrate something? If people in the meeting are not focused and contributing, your company will be wasting valuable time and money. Make sure each meeting has a common focus, allows for open communication, and is void of personal attacks. Each participant should have clearly defined roles and responsibilities. The meeting should have the right participants, be held in the right place, and occur at the right time. Here is a checklist for conducting an effective meeting:

Before the meeting:
- Give appropriate notice
- Send objectives of the meeting in advance
- Prepare charts, graphs, overheads, and handouts
- Give participants material in advance, if appropriate
- Arrive early to set up the room the way you want it

During the meeting:
- State the objectives and check for understanding
- Establish ground rules for questions, breaks, and interruptions
- Cut the chit-chat
- Don't serve food

- Limit your talking and solicit feedback from participants
- Don't evaluate or judge comments during the meeting
- Summarize all major points before continuing onto something else
- Ask open-ended questions to stimulate dialogue
- Limit committees
- Intervene when necessary to keep people on the agenda
- Have someone responsible for recording ideas
- Schedule when the next meeting will be held

After the meeting:
- Send out results of decisions that were made during the meeting
- Follow up on action items
- Clarify any misunderstandings
- Check on the progress of participants if you delegated to them
- Create and send out minutes of meeting, if appropriate

A meeting that is properly planned and implemented can be a very effective tool for increasing productivity. A good meeting enhances communication among attendees. Good communication is an essential ingredient to successful companies.

Life-Work Compass

Principle Five:
Manage Multiple Priorities

What
1. Focus on things you have control over.
2. Eliminate your biggest time-wasters.
3. Prioritize activities by what's urgent and important.
4. Delegate responsibility *and* authority.
5. Manage meetings effectively.

When
1. At all times in your life and career.
2. Do it now.
3. Do this every time you prepare your "to do" list.
4. At the time a delegated task is discussed.
5. Every time you conduct or attend a meeting.

Why
1. Because those are the things you can do something about.
2. So they stop controlling your available time.
3. To make sure you stay focused on high-impact activities.
4. Because it helps to create trust.
5. So you don't waste your time or the time of others.

How
1. By being aware of what the controllable items are to begin with.
2. By completing the time-waster action plan.
3. By identifying which quadrant the activity belongs in.
4. By clearly discussing the levels of authority with others.
5. By creating an agenda and sticking with it.

Play the Team Game

Getting ahead in today's business world is not easy. Whether a company employs you or you work for yourself, you must manage your career. There are limited resources. Competing for jobs, money, time, material, equipment, the attention of the boss, and recognition from peers is challenging.

Networking is one way to meet the challenge. Networking means managing the relationships you have in your personal life and professional career in a way that promotes a win-win outcome. Think of networking as a way of planting seeds. The more seeds you plant, the more opportunity exists.

My wife and I both belong to the Naperville (Illinois) Chamber of Commerce. We received invitations to attend a holiday party at the home of a person with whom my wife works. So, with a bottle of wine and hors d' oeuvres in hand, we decided to go. Other Chamber employees were there with their spouses, many of whom I didn't know too well. So I made my rounds, introducing myself to them. When one of the spouses asked me what I did for a living, I told him that I conducted training programs for companies on various subjects. When I asked him what he did for a living, he told me he was the Human Resources director for a financial company in Chicago. One thing led to another, and within three weeks he scheduled me to conduct some seminars for his employees. I encourage you to attend after-hour functions where you can meet people. You never know when an opportunity will present itself!

Today's workplace is uncertain and ever-changing. Things will not always go as planned in your life and career. Your life can change when you least expect it. Planting seeds along the way can make the unexpected less painful. Consider some of the following trends:

- Downsizing continues. Companies like to run lean. There are fewer management jobs available than in the past, and these jobs probably won't return.
- Competition comes from developing countries. More companies are turning to cheap labor in an effort to reduce production costs.
- Less loyalty. There's no such thing as job security. People who think their jobs are secure are fooling themselves.
- Fierce competition for fewer promotions. The people who have managed to survive downsizing are facing fewer promotion opportunities. Seniority doesn't matter much anymore.
- Job-hopping on the rise. Career paths are difficult to plan. People are frequently changing jobs.
- Growth in small businesses. Discouraged by corporate limitations, many people are now starting their own businesses.

Promoting yourself inside your company is necessary for your career growth. This can be done easily once you know the language.

Understanding the PIP Formula
The difference between being relatively successful in your career versus being very successful in your career is your understanding of, and your ability to, "play the game." Being able to "play the game" means understanding your company's culture and internal workings. It means understanding the "unwritten" rules that are often unspoken but nonetheless important. It means being a team player and going with the flow while at the same time not compromising your personal values or integrity. In a word, it means understanding your company's "politics."

When people hear the word "politics," they usually cringe. That's because the word provokes a negative connotation for most people. When you ask people if they "play politics" inside their company, most people respond with an emphatic "no," because they feel it's a bad thing to do. However, understanding the political structure of your company and then operating successfully within that structure can make your career. If you don't know how to play the game, your ignorance will hurt your career. Knowing what to do and what not to do is critical to your career success, no matter what company you work for. The "game" of playing smart politics can be fun, exciting, and very rewarding.

Most people learn company politics the hard way—by making mistakes and then hearing about how they messed up. There is no course in any university that teaches students the art of understanding company politics. If you aspire to get ahead in your company, you must learn how the game is played and then determine how to play it within the boundaries of your personal values. Playing the game within the boundaries means behaving in a way that does not compromise your personal values as you are doing what is ethical and right. This means not being a "brown-noser" or a "yes person." Being politically savvy means being smart without being cute.

To help you understand company politics, I introduce you to what I call the PIP formula: the first "P" stands for productivity; the "I" stands for image; and the second "P" stands for participation. Knowing how to incorporate these three objectives into your daily work can be a great boost to your career.

Productivity
Image
Participation

Productivity means achieving desired results in your job, meeting your goals, hitting the production numbers, coming in on budget and on schedule. Productivity can be measured rather easily in most organizations by looking at such things as numbers, percentages, or dollar amounts. Counting and reporting results on charts and graphs is one way that management measures your productivity.

Your job description is a good starting point for understanding what is expected of you. A good job description lists the duties, responsibilities, and outcomes that are expected of you in your job. If you don't have a formal job description, then you must rely on your managers to communicate what results they expect from you. Even if you do have a written job description, you must still rely on your boss to communicate the results he or she expects from you. Many people indicate that they aren't sure what is expected of them in their jobs. You must be crystal clear about what is expected of you! Not knowing, or assuming what your boss wants, can get you into a great deal of trouble. You must know *exactly* what is expected of you in your job. Don't rely on your job description only, and don't assume anything.

Do you know what is expected of you right now in your job? List here the top three things that your boss expects from you this month:

_____

_____

_____

As you look at the things that you listed, make sure there is nothing that is vague or unclear. Are there specific numbers and due dates associated with the items you listed? Statements like "do the best you can," and "as soon as possible," are not specific and are open to interpretation. Taking a few extra minutes to clarify expectations before you start the project or task can save you valuable time in the long run. Your responsibility is to get the job done on time and within budget in order to meet expectations. If you're not sure—ask. If the person you ask is not sure— then find out. There is no room for being vague here. You have to know what's expected, and then do what it takes to make it happen. Sometimes this means doing a little after-hours legwork to research what your internal and external customers want. Taking the time in the short run to find out what is expected can pay nice dividends in the long run. There is no excuse for not doing your homework.

Most companies measure job performance in terms of *quality* and *quantity*. *Quality* can be simply defined as meeting requirements. Whose requirements? The customer's. Keep in mind that customers can either be internal or external. Your boss is your customer too. *Quantity* simply means how much or how many. Understanding quality and quantity requirements helps you identify what is expected of you in terms of productivity—the first "P" in the PIP formula.

Image. Getting results, however, is not enough. You need to accomplish those results in the right way. That's where your image comes into play. Image is the way in which you are perceived or regarded in your company. Your image is what comes to mind when your name is mentioned at your company. How and what do people think about you? Your image can have a "make or break" impact on your career. Keep in mind that whenever you interact with another person, that person is mentally asking two questions: "Do I like you?" and "Can I trust you?" The answer to these two questions is how people perceive you. Keep in mind that a person's perception is their reality. This perceived reality could be good or bad, positive or negative, true or untrue. You want to do everything possible to create and maintain a positive image in your company.

In the following space, list two people whom you think have a positive image and two people whom you think have a negative image in your company.

Positive-image people: **Negative-image people:**

_____   _____

_____   _____

Now ask yourself, what made you list these people in the categories that you did? Why do you feel the way you do about the positive image people and the negative image people? If others in your company had to put you in one of the two categories, what category would they would put you in? If you think that your image could use some improvement or if your image is not what you would like it to be, then you might want to repair your reputation and enhance your image:

• *Do what you say you will do.* Anytime you make a commitment to someone else, you must fulfill that commitment on time, every time. If you can't do what you said you were going to do, then you must immediately inform other people as to why you can't meet their expectations and then come up with alternatives.

• *Be "other oriented."* Think first of other people and how you can meet their needs, not yours. I know many people who think of themselves first and others second. Switch this thinking around by putting others' needs first and your needs second.

• *Go above and beyond what is expected.* Sometimes, just meeting others' expectations is not enough. If your image is tarnished, then you must go above and beyond what is expected. This will speed up the repair process and put you in good graces with others.

• *Don't wait to be asked.* Take the initiative and do what needs to be done without being asked. If you see something that needs to be organized, organize it. Clean out the file cabinets, supply closet, or storeroom. People will notice and appreciate your efforts.

• *Leave the company.* Sometimes, your image and reputation is just too badly damaged to repair. No matter what you do, people will still think of your blunders when they think of you. If that is the case, you might want to think about moving on.

Participation. Another way to enhance your image is through participation. Participation means involving yourself in as many opportunities as practical within your company. This is the second "P" in the PIP formula. For example, you might: volunteer for projects, join a committee or task force, make a presentation at the next meeting, play on the company's sports team, or attend an after-hours function. Participation means being "plugged in" to your company and doing things outside your company. For example, you might volunteer your time to help a local or national charity, stay after hours to plan a party for someone who is retiring, or work on an annual event sponsored by your company. Being a willing and active participant in such things will impact your career in a positive way. It's a good way of letting your company know that you are a "player." Understanding your company's culture is a prerequisite for climbing the corporate ladder. Not understanding company politics or not wanting to play the game will definitely get you plateaued in your career.

Many people make the mistake of focusing on their job productivity only. Having good numbers and operating within budget is not enough. You might volunteer for overtime occasionally, choose to be a part of things when asked, or volunteer for something before you are asked.

By doing more than what is expected, by exceeding expectations and meeting deadlines, you become known as a person who can be trusted with responsibility.

To give you an example of the PIP formula in action, suppose that you are the accountant for a non-profit organization and are responsible for producing the financial report for the upcoming finance committee meeting. Members of the finance committee are prominent city leaders. The meeting is scheduled for Tuesday morning at 8 a.m. Your boss, using the information on your report, will be making recommendations to the committee for a much-needed building project in your city. The finance committee will then make a formal proposal to the mayor so she can announce her decision for the project at the press conference scheduled for the following Wednesday.

The computers have been down since the Thursday before the meeting, and they aren't up and running until 4 p.m. on Friday afternoon. The finance committee is meeting for the sole purpose of approving the final budget for the new building. Not getting the report done is not an option. Giving the report to your boss at 7:30 a.m. on Tuesday morning does not give him enough time to review the information on the report. What do you do?

Based on the PIP formula, meeting minimum requirements here is not enough. Regardless of your weekend plans, you need to work over the weekend to get the report done so your boss has it in his hands by Monday morning. Why? So he can review the information and properly prepare for Tuesday's meeting.

Not having the report to present to the committee causes a ripple effect that will make you, your boss, and the committee look bad. This ripple will turn into a tidal wave of problems for the mayor and the city. Who do you think will be blamed for not meeting expectations?

When you combine all three elements of the PIP formula—Performance, Image, and Participation—you can make a good name for yourself and be known as a team player. When your name is mentioned, you will definitely be seen in a positive light.

Networking at Different Levels

There is a unique and distinct language spoken at the different levels in any organization, and I'm not thinking about Spanish, French, or German. It is an unspoken language. You need to learn and use this language if you are to advance within your organization. Your career success depends on knowing what "silent language" is spoken in your organization. Again this knowledge has to be learned on the job—sometimes, the hard way.

What do I mean by "speaking the language?" Consider the following examples: union people speak union language, staff people speak staff language, supervisors speak supervisor language, managers speak manager language, and presidents speak president language. People tend to interact mainly with people who work at their same level. Why? Because they all speak the same language.

We've all had the experience of interacting with another group of people and feeling uncomfortable. It takes time to get a feel for who the players are. Have you ever joined a group that was very different from the group that you normally interact with? Perhaps you felt a little awkward. That's because you were not yet comfortable with the protocol at that level. What's acceptable and what's not has to be learned, usually by observing the behavioral norms of the group. That's how society functions.

Consider the following things that people own, belong to, or have done:

Belong to a country club	Belong to a health club
Own a Harley-Davidson	Own a snowmobile
Skydive	Own a four-wheel drive truck
Play on a softball team	Belong to a bowling league
Belong to a golf league	Belong to a frequent-flyer club
Manage something	Belong to the Republican party
Belong to a union	Belong to the Democratic party
Own a minivan	Drive a sports utility vehicle
Serve in the military	Participate in civic activities

To belong to any of these groups, own any of these things, or experience any of these activities means being a part of that particular culture. If you don't ride a Harley-Davidson motorcycle, for example, you won't understand that culture and won't relate to those who do.

When approaching other people for the first time, consider the following tips that will help you integrate into the group:

1. *Just say "hello."* It's a very simple way to greet people.

2. *Remember people's names.* Try to remember other people's names. It's the quickest way to establish rapport with them. In his book *How to Win Friends and Influence People*, Dale Carnagie wrote: "The sweetest sound to a person's ear is his name."

3. *Introduce peers to each other, one by one, by name.* Acknowledge everyone in the group. Don't assume that everyone knows each other. If you're not sure, then ask.

4. *Introduce a superior to a subordinate.* Say the name of the superior first: "Tom (your boss), I'd like you to meet Al Smith. Al, this is my boss, Tom."

5. *Introduce a customer to people in your company.* Treat customers and clients as superiors. Use their names first when introducing them to other people in your company.

6. ***Stand up when shaking hands.*** Always greet people—male and female alike—with a professional handshake. Greet all people the same.

7. ***Reflect on the occasion.*** Know why you are there, and then feel free to chitchat about the occasion.

8. ***Find areas of common interest.*** Start by asking questions about the other person's interests. Comment on what they say and stay in their world.

9. ***Don't talk about religion or politics.*** That's a good way to alienate yourself. A good rule of thumb is to avoid those topics.

10. ***Invite other people to join your group.*** If you are going to do something, try inviting other people to join you. They will tell you if they want to join you or not. It's a good way to make them feel welcome.

Remember, in order to grow, you must leave your comfort zone. This means being open to meeting new people and doing new things. Exposing yourself to new and different things can be very exciting. Look for opportunities to network at different levels. For example, if you play in the company's annual golf outing and always golf with the same people, try joining a different foursome. It's a great way to meet new people in an informal setting. Or try going out to lunch with a new group of people. Always being with the same people might be comfortable, but you miss an opportunity to grow.

Approaching Your Boss

Never approach your boss with a problem without having a solution. When you inform your boss of a problem your boss will likely ask you, "What do *you* think *you* should do about it?" If you don't have any ideas, you will quickly become part of the problem and not the solution. Doing this often will tarnish your image.

You don't have to have "the" solution to your problem before you approach your boss; however, you need to do your homework before you approach your boss. You must have some alternative solutions. For example, if you inform your boss that your co-worker called in sick, you might suggest having another co-worker step in to fill customer orders and get them shipped on time. Having a solution to the problem before you talk to your boss helps to make you look good.

Another powerful way to approach your boss is what I call the "third-party" approach. It means deflecting your conversation to a third party so if the boss disagrees with you, he is disagreeing with someone or something else, not you personally.

Once I was invited to attend a meeting with the chairman of the board and his staff at a major mid-western hospital. This hospital was merging with another hospital, and they were considering conducting several training sessions to help their employees through the transition. During the meeting, the chairman asked me how I thought he should proceed. Using the third-party approach, I said, "Based on my experience working with other healthcare providers, I feel that you should . . ." The other healthcare providers, in this case, represented the "third-party." So, if the chairman disagreed with what I said, he would be disagreeing with my experience with other hospitals and not with me personally. This approach deflects the "I disagree with you" situation onto the third party.

You can use this technique with your boss by saying the following: "Based on what I hear our customers say, I think we should . . . ." "Based on what our competition is doing, I think that we should . . . ." "Based on what they are doing in another department, perhaps we could. . . ." This technique tells your boss that you've done your homework and have investigated other options and possibilities. It also suggests that you have been looking at the big picture and not just your department. It means that you have thought about solutions to the problem. This is an outstanding way to enhance your reputation as a problem-solver in your organization. What a great way to enhance your image!

Being a Team Player

So much is written about being a "team player" these days. Yet despite all the talk about a team effort, many people have never had a true team experience. People can work in the same department for years, serve on committees, meet in management groups regularly, and still not be part of a team. Instead, they are part of a group of people who come together occasionally to work together. This does not mean, however, that they are working together as a team. Here are some fundamental differences between a work group and a team:

Group	Team
People rely on the leader.	People share leadership roles.
People work individually.	People work with others.
People wait for decisions.	People collaborate together.
People are independent.	People are interdependent.
People have hidden conflicts.	People work out their differences.

A team-based organization is one that uses a team as its basic work unit for things such as planning, decision-making, and completing the work. A high-performance team is made up of dedicated people who share a common set of values and have a high degree of trust in each other. A good example would be a professional sports team who wins the World Series or Super Bowl. Teams do not make it to this level if they do not have good coaches and players and are dedicated to winning. All players have a job to do, and they know how to do it. The same holds true for today's business teams.

Your job is to use your talents to achieve results for your organization by effectively serving your customers, whomever they may be. You do this by identifying the needs of your customers and then serving them to the best of your ability. However, you cannot do this alone. You must rely on people in your own department and coordinate with people in other departments. Interdependence means working with and through other people to accomplish team or organizational goals.

If you are currently serving on a project team, you must know what your role is on that team. Why are you on the team? What is expected of you? What do you bring to the table? What is your expertise? Here are 10 ideas for how you can help your team reach its goals:

1. Initiate action. Be the person who helps the team get started. You want to be known as the person who is not afraid to move forward. This is leadership in action. Encourage others to follow your lead and support your initiative.

2. Seek the opinions of others. Be the person who includes others by asking for their opinion or suggestion. Asking, not telling, is a good way to show that you care about others and value their ideas. Seeking the opinions of others is a good way to build a team.

3. Clarify what was said. Be the person who restates and summarizes the facts. Reflective listening means putting what was said in your own words: "So if I understand you correctly Jim, you feel that we should . . . ."

4. Offer alternative ideas. Be the person who comes up with creative alternatives. Don't stop at just one or two alternatives. Try to come up with several different ideas and alternative solutions. Sometimes the best idea is the next one.

5. Move toward consensus. Be the person who helps the team move toward resolution. This does not mean 100 percent agreement or majority rules. Consensus means that team members support the decision, even if they don't agree with it.

6. Keep communication channels open. Be the person who makes sure information is shared freely and with the proper people. There's nothing more frustrating than being the last person to know what's going on. Team members look out for each other and keep each other in the loop at all times.

7. Compromise when necessary. Be the person who is willing to adjust your ideas for the sake of the team, giving in to someone else's idea for the purpose of serving the customer better. Try not to let your ego get the best of you.

8.   Encourage others. Be the person who encourages others to get involved and contribute their best thinking. Everyone should offer their ideas during team meetings.

9.   Relieve tension. Be the person who lightens up the conversation when two or more team members disagree with each other. Some conflict is normal; however, there comes a time when someone should interject a lighter comment to break the tension between team members. Never use humor at the expense of team member's feelings.

10. Promote harmony. Be the person who is friendly and warm in response to others on the team. Always extend an open hand and an open heart. Remember, these people are members of your team. Try to promote a feeling of unity.

By using the PIP formula, networking with others, and approaching your boss with alternatives, you will create a reputation as a team player. And, if you do these things for the ultimate purpose of serving the customer, you will make a positive name for yourself.

Life-Work Compass

Principle Six:
Play the Team Game

What?

1. Play the "team" game.
2. Apply the PIP formula.
3. Network at different levels.
4. Approach your boss with power.
5. Be known as a team player.

Why?

1. Because it will help your career.
2. Because productivity alone is not enough.
3. Because it gets you noticed throughout the organization.
4. Because it shows that you've done your homework.
5. Because everyone likes a team player.

How?

1. By participating in internal and external company events.
2. By discussing expectations with your boss in terms of results and behaviors.
3. By approaching other people when appropriate.
4. By offering possible solutions to your problems.
5. By volunteering for projects and committees.

When?

1. When you work with others in your organization.
2. At the beginning of any new assignment or task.
3. When you face an opportunity, especially after hours.
4. Anytime you approach your boss with a problem.
5. Always.

Be Open to Change

Select Your Information

Every day we are bombarded with information through various media—the Internet, television news shows, newspapers and magazines—as well as from other sources. The immense increase in the daily information that is available to us today should cause us to change how we select and process that information.

While it is important to keep up with current events, we must choose what information we wish to receive and how we wish to receive it. Advertisers inundate us with so many commercials to entice us to buy their products that it sometime seems that the actual news is just a vehicle for the advertisers. A 30-minute segment of network news consists of just 22 minutes of reporting and eight minutes commercials. That's a lot of advertisement for "new and improved" product coming at you in such a short period of time. With all the commercials, no wonder people like to channel surf.

Advertisers compete fiercely for your attention. They invest big budgets to entice you to buy their products. Just think of how much "junk mail" you receive every day. Now, advertisers are sending "junk e-mail." As your name appears on more and more mailing lists and data bases, you receive more and more messages. So, what should you do with all the data and information you are exposed to these days?

First, be selective in what you read. At work, definitely read everything on your company's Web site. Know what's on it and why your company is sending that information. How often is the

Website changed? Who changes it? There's nothing more embarrassing than when an external customer knows more about your company than you do. When this happens, customers are usually more than happy to tell you all about your company. Some of them get a kick out of knowing more than you. To help you avoid this embarrassment, you should read any and all publications that your company puts out. This includes brochures, pamphlets, advertisements, and news releases.

Read only the mail that is addressed to you personally. Just because you receive something in the mail doesn't mean that you should automatically read it. How many e-mail messages do you receive daily? Some people receive so many messages that they could spend the entire day just reading them and writing responses. Don't send your e-mail message to people who don't need to receive it. Also, be brief. Say what you need to say—and then end it. Other people's time is valuable too. Make your message short and to the point.

The people who are successful in today's information overload society, have the ability to navigate around informational "black holes." These can drown you in non-essential information and waste your time and energy. Remember three things when it comes to handling information: 1) Be selective in what you read, 2) come to a conclusion on what is being communicated, and then 3) act on that information.

Information overload is just one of the many challenges we need to face. Just as we can develop strategies to handle all this new information, we can find effective ways to approach any situation that requires a transition from the old to the new.

The Challenge of Transition

In his book *Managing Transitions,* William Bridges says, "It isn't the change that does you in, it's the transition." Transition is the "in-between" period from the old to the new. It is the process of "letting go" of something and moving to a "new beginning." Transition is seldom easy. It means completely and absolutely leaving the old situation behind. If you are unwilling to let go of the past, transition to the new beginning cannot take place.

Henry Wadsworth Longfellow said, "Great is the art of beginning, but greater is the art of ending." Letting go of the past is very difficult for many people because it means leaving behind something that is familiar. However, hanging on to the past will keep you from growing and reaching your potential. Transition begins when you leave the old situation behind. The person who is successful in today's society is the person who learns how to "end" things and move on.

Transition has three phases:
1. Letting go of the past.
2. The in-between period.
3. The new beginning.

Successfully managing change means successfully managing transition. In this case, we're talking about the process of leaving the old behind, going through a period of uncertainty, and then moving on to a new beginning. It is a process that flows over time from one phase to the next with many adjustments along the way. Often, this process is difficult, frustrating, and scary. Even when we determine that the change is good for us, transition can be challenging.

During the best of times, transition can be long and difficult. During times of national disasters, it can be devastating. This is no more evident than in the wake of the terrorist attack on the World Trade Center in New York and the Pentagon near Washington D.C. Both attacks happened in a brief moment in time; however, the transition will take months, if not years. Our lives have been changed forever as a result of the tragic events that took place on September 11, 2001. Hopefully, those events will mark the beginning of a movement toward coming together rather than pulling apart.

Managing the "In-between" Phase

The in-between phase of transition is when you are neither here nor there—you are somewhere between the old and the new. This period is most uncomfortable for many people. It is a time filled with high emotion and uncertainty when we ask, "Am I doing the right thing?" On the other hand, it is also a time filled with great opportunity for those who boldly go forward. Making the transition from one thing to the next or from one place to the next can be frightening. However, in order to grow as human beings, we must resolve to move forward. It's a good thing, not a bad thing.

Failing to understand the transition process and underestimating its impact are two of the biggest problems that people face in managing change. Many companies do a relatively good job at introducing change but a terrible job at managing transition. Many times, managers announce that, "Starting Monday, we're going with self-directed work teams." They fail to realize that they must manage the transition period between the old way and the new beginning. Most managers don't know how to manage transitions. They are taught to "make it happen," "get results," and "do it now." They are rewarded for achieving real-time results, not for managing the in-between period of transition.

Transition is a messy time when people's emotions run high and resistance is great. Management typically does a poor job of articulating the new situation. They use vague generalizations when announcing change: "We need to work smarter, not harder." "We need to tighten our belts." "We need to do more with less." These vague statements do little to inspire employees. That's why most employees view the "major announcement" as just another fad They say to themselves, "This too will pass."

What's happening in your life? What are you are experiencing now that represents an "in-between" time? Things like getting married, having a baby, starting a new job, buying a new house, or even driving a new car all represent change. In the following space, list some changes that you have experienced where you had to let go of the past:

_____

_____

_____

_____

Now look at your list. How are you doing with letting go of the past? Are you making a smooth transition? Are you moving forward? If you are reluctant to let go of the old way, do you think it will hold you back?

If you feel like you're stuck, setting a deadline as an endpoint will help liberate you. For example, if you're not happy with your current job and would like to find another job, set a deadline for yourself. You might say, "If nothing improves in my current situation six months from today, I will start sending out my resume." Now you have an end point to help you with a new beginning.

A transition to a new beginning starts by letting go of the past. Managing the in-between period during transition is essential to your success. This is a time for patience, perseverance, and the courage of your convictions. Following are some suggestions for managing transition:

- Identify what no longer has value and meaning for you.
- Let go of things that hold you back.
- Set meaningful, future-oriented goals.
- Boldly go forward into a new beginning.

Why People Resist Change

People resist change for one simple reason—fear! Fear is the single most important reason why people fail to reach their full potential in life. Fear of the unknown and fear of giving up something are more common reasons why many people are reluctant to leave their current situation. Failure to enter the in-between period means not moving through transition and into the new beginning. In baseball, you can't steal second base with one foot stuck on first. You have to leave first base to get to second. You may get called out or you might be safe. It's the chance you have to take.

Controlling Your Fear

You start controlling your fears by first identifying them. In her book *Feel the Fear And Do It Anyway,* Dr. Susan Jeffers writes, "At the bottom of every fear is simply the fear that you can't handle whatever life may bring you." The fear of looking like a fool, being laughed at, or being ridiculed by others are major reasons why people don't venture out into the unknown. Many times, people don't know what they are afraid of; they just know that "it's scary out there." Success means taking risks. Taking risks can be scary. Being scared is not a bad thing—it's normal. Identifying your fears and then effectively dealing with them will increase your chance of becoming successful and reaching your potential.

To reduce your fears and take risks, you must have a strong belief that you can handle any situation that comes your way. The willingness to take calculated risks is a trait of most successful people. Having confidence in yourself and moving forward will help you reach your potential. Franklin D. Roosevelt said, "The only thing we have to fear, is fear itself."

Think about something you currently want to do but are afraid to do, for whatever reason. Ask yourself: "What's the worst thing that can happen to me?" Identifying this worst thing will help you reduce your fears and leave the old situation behind.

In the following space, list some things that you would like to have, do, or be in your life but are afraid to have, do, or become:

Things I would like to have in my life:

_____

_____

_____

_____

Things I would like to do in my life:

_____

_____

_____

_____

Things I would like to become in my life:

_____

_____

_____

_____

Now ask, "What's the worst that can happen if things don't work out?" Sometimes, just by identifying the worst-case scenario, you can greatly reduce your fears. Even though you may experience a certain degree of failure, you can handle it. Having a strong belief in yourself that you can handle whatever comes your way will help reduce your fears.

Four Phases of Change

Change happens! Your life is one continuous process of evolving. What you evolve toward is up to you. Whether you like it or not, your life and your company are constantly changing. When people go through change, they typically will move through the four phases of change: 1) confusion, 2) defiance, 3) investigation, and 4) acceptance. Skill, knowledge, and productivity typically drop during the four phases. The curved line in the following diagram represents what happens to the average person's knowledge, skill, and productivity levels during change.

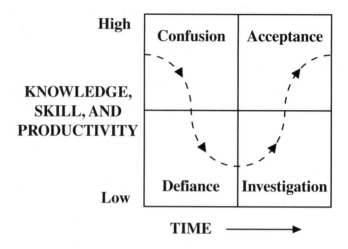

When change is introduced, people struggle to figure out exactly what the change will bring. Since the future is unknown, change can represent an uncertain time. Most people react by assessing "What's in it for me?" "How will these events change my life?" "What will I now have to do differently as a result of these events?" "What can I do to help others?" Many people are now asking these questions in the wake of the terrorist attacks.

When change is announced at work, most employees don't understand what the change will mean for them. *Confusion* is typically the first feeling that employees experience when change is introduced. Employees wander around asking each other questions. Misunderstanding and misinterpretation of what was said normally cause knowledge, skill, and productivity to drop during this phase.

After the initial announcements, people try to imagine how the new situation will look or what the change will mean once it is in place. If people determine that the change will not be good for them, they typically move from a state of *confusion* to one of *defiance*. Here, they may say, "No way," "It won't work," or "This is stupid." They may deeply resent the change initiative. Productivity, at this stage, is at its lowest. This is a very frustrating time for most employees.

Over time, most employees will move into the *investigation* phase. Once they understand that the change will not go away, they begin dealing with the new situation. They might say, "What the heck," or "Okay, I'll take a look at it, but I'm not going to like it." Most employees realize that they must move forward and explore the new situation. During this phase, knowledge, skill, and productivity start to climb again.

Over time, most employees will move into the *acceptance* phase. Productivity during this phase starts to climb and may even surpass old productivity levels, which should be the whole purpose of the change in the first place. Why introduce change if it does not improve some aspect of serving the customer? Sometimes, employees really like the new changes. They may say, "Wow, I actually like this new stuff," and "I'll never go back to the old way."

Some employees, however, simply can't accept the new situation and choose to leave the company. This is not necessarily a bad thing, because those people tend to drag others down. When they leave the company, try not to talk critically about them. They are only doing what they feel is best for them.

Management Mistakes

Since most managers aren't trained to handle change, they typically don't know how to deal with all the emotional responses they get from their employees when the company announces change. Managers are typically rated on productivity and other performance measures, not on how they deal with people's emotional behavior during change. Many senior managers won't take the time to deal with people's emotions during change because they are under pressure to keep production at current levels. However, not taking the time to address their staff's emotional reaction to change is a big mistake!

Since managers are measured by numbers, budgets, and bottom-lines, they tend to focus on those things and not on the feelings of their employees. They care about their employees, but they are pressured by upper management to keep production levels high and get the product out the door on time while not compromising quality.

As managers push their employees to work longer and harder to get the numbers back to acceptable levels, they start to see low morale, bad attitudes, further production drops, and ultimately employee turnover. So, what can be done?

First you need to understand the situation for what it is, and try to find ways to be helpful. Focus on how you can contribute, not on what makes you mad and how you can "get back" at the company. Keep in mind that the pain of transition is temporary.

Recommendations to Consider During Change

Here are some recommendations that you may want to consider during each phase of the change process. You can pick and choose the things you feel are best for you, or you can come up with your own ideas as a result of these suggestions. In either case, feel free to try different things during change. The main thing is to take action.

During the *confusion* phase:
- Ask why the change is necessary.
- Ask your boss to be as specific as possible.
- Ask why the company feels this change is important.
- Ask how the change will affect the customer.
- Get as much information as possible.

During the *defiance* phase:
- Tell others how you feel about the change.
- Let your boss know about your concerns.
- Don't be afraid to express your feelings.
- Don't feel like you have to "show no fear."
- Ask your boss to address your concerns.
- Request updates on how things are going.

During the *investigation* phase:
- Set short-term goals (daily/weekly).
- Ask for training to update your skills.
- Volunteer to be trained in the initial wave.
- Communicate and brainstorm new ideas with your co-workers.
- Show that you are willing to be a part of the change.

During the *acceptance* phase:
- Set long-term goals (monthly/quarterly).
- Conduct planning sessions with others.
- Reinforce people who are responding to the change.
- Be a model for the others.

Rebuilding Trust

Developing trusting relationships is always a good thing to do. An environment of trust is especially essential during a period of intense change. One way to establish a relationship of trust with others is to communicate in an open and honest manner with all people at all times. Playing games with hidden agendas is never a good idea. People will eventually discover what you're up to and will not trust you completely. Try to operate in ways that are mutually beneficial to both parties. Creating common ground of open and honest communication is good for everyone. Do what's in the best interest for both parties.

When people trust their managers and trust that together they can carry out change, they are likely to undertake change even if it frightens or frustrates them. When people don't trust their managers, they are likely to avoid or resist change.

You can enhance or reduce the trust in your company by what you say and what you do. To increase your trustworthiness: Do what you say you will do! If you make a commitment to another person, you must keep it. Not doing so will hurt your credibility and reputation. If you can't keep an obligation, explain why and offer alternatives.

Change can be seen as either a threat or an opportunity. Successful people see change as an opportunity to grow and improve. Try to be the kind of person who helps others move through transition and onto a new and wonderful beginning.

Life-Work Compass

Principle Seven:
Be Open to Change

What?

1. Handle information overload.
2. Let go of the past.
3. Control your fear.
4. Move through the four phases of change.
5. Do what you say you will do.

Why?

1. If you don't, it will handle you.
2. It's the starting point for transition.
3. To help you reach your potential.
4. To help you deal with today's changes.
5. To foster trust during change.

How?

1. By being selective in what you read.
2. By setting goals and looking forward.
3. By identifying the worse-case scenario.
4. By being aware of the symptoms of the four phases.
5. By acting on all commitments and following up.

When?

1. Every day.
2. Any time you are faced with major change.
3. When you seem stuck and are afraid.
4. During any change situation.
5. Always!

Create a Positive Attitude

Examining Your Attitude

Once a manager was dispatched to determine how laborers felt about their work. He went to a building site in France. He approached the first worker and asked, "What are you doing?" "What, are you blind?" the worker snapped back. "I'm cutting these rocks with primitive tools and putting them together the way the boss tells me . . . it's back-breaking, boring work" The dispatcher quickly moved to a second worker. He asked the same question: "What are you doing?" The worker replied, "I'm shaping these rocks into forms that are then assembled according to the architect's plans. It's hard work, but I earn five francs a week. Things could be worse." The dispatcher went on to the third worker. "And what are you doing?" he asked. "Why, can't you see?" said the worker as he lifted his arms to the sky. "I'm building a cathedral!"

This story exemplifies different attitudes and outlooks. Attitudes can be either positive or negative, depending on how you perceive the events in your life. Successful people have a positive outlook, even when the chips are down.

An attitude can be defined as the way a person chooses to respond to a given stimulus. That stimulus can be a person, place, thing, or situation. Everyone has an attitude. It can be good, bad, or neutral. Most people don't give it much thought as they go about their daily lives. However, I'd like you to think about your attitude. On a scale from 1 to 10, with 10 being high, how would you rate your overall attitude?

lousy		poor		fair		good		very good		excellent
1	2	3	4	5	6	7	8	9	10

What or who determines your attitude? Where does your attitude come from and how is it formed? How does your attitude affect the results in your life or do you think it really doesn't have that much impact at all? Do you think people with positive attitudes are more successful in life than others, or do you think they are just lucky? How significant is your attitude to your success? These are good questions that actually have been studied and researched over the years by hundreds of people.

It's been said that attitude, more than anything else, will determine how successful you will be in your life. Do you agree? In the 1930's, the Carnagie Foundation surveyed hundreds of people and asked them what percentage of success is determined by one's attitude and what percent by skill and knowledge? The study found that 85 percent of a person's success is determined by attitude; 15 percent by skill and knowledge. When the survey was repeated in the 1980's, the numbers were found to be the same. Having a positive attitude is critical to your success.

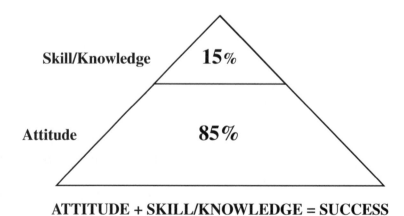

ATTITUDE + SKILL/KNOWLEDGE = SUCCESS

What exactly does *success* mean? I define *success* as the progressive and consistent movement toward a meaningful goal. A *meaningful goal*, by the way, is one that you set for yourself, not one that someone else sets for you, and one that impacts your life in a positive way.

Your success depends on what you identify is good for you, not what others say should be good for you. Constantly comparing your achievements to those of others, or defining success from their point of view, is not in your best interest. Success is whatever you say it is. You must decide what success should look like for you. Once you do so, stick to your convictions, no matter what anyone else says or thinks. Persistence is what separates successful people from unsuccessful people.

Eliminate the "Entitlement" Mentality

One thing that will negatively impact your image are comments such as "You owe me" or "I think I deserve . . ." These comments, when made over and over, can be very damaging to your career. This is what I call the "entitlement mentality." Successful people do not keep score on everything that happens or doesn't happen to them. No one owes you anything, no matter how deserving you think you are. Demanding that you be compensated or rewarded for something is a great way to tarnish your relationship with others.

If people get paid every two weeks, consider that paycheck as a way the company "gets even" with its employees (in a positive way) after a two-week period. This is how it works: First, the employees work two weeks and accumulate some credit for the time they spend doing work. Second, the company gives them a paycheck for the work they did during that two-week time period. Third, when they accept that paycheck, they are now "even" with their employer. They have been paid for their services. I hear so many people whine about having seniority over other people, as if that alone entitles them to whatever they think they deserve. Not so. A person doesn't have 27 years of seniority; they have 27 years of being even! Remember, your company "gets even" with you every time you accept your paycheck.

Responsible and successful people don't waste time keeping track of who owes them. Successful people reciprocate good deeds on their own because it's the right thing to do. Having a mentality of entitlement, no matter how proficient you are in your job, will eventually hurt you in your career. Don't waste time keeping score. Instead, spend your time in the service of others. You'll be surprised how many people will come to your aid when you have a positive attitude. People like to be around individuals with positive attitudes. Consider this diagram:

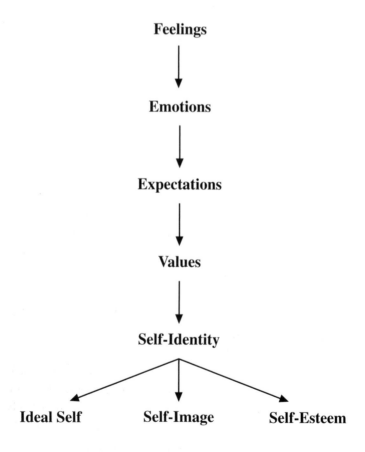

Feelings

Emotions

Expectations

Values

Self-Identity

Ideal Self   **Self-Image**   **Self-Esteem**

Where Do Attitudes Come From?

Where do attitudes come from, and how are they formed? Attitudes are formed from a person's values, beliefs, and expectations. Every event that happens to you affects you in some way. All of those events combine to help you form your attitude.

The three parts that help to make up your self-identity are 1) your ideal self, 2) your self-image and 3) your self-esteem.

Think of your *ideal self* as your hero. Ideally, who would you like to be like? Who influenced you the most in your life? This could be a parent, grandparent, someone in sports, or school. It is someone who has made a positive impact in your life, someone you look up to. In the following space, list three people who have influenced your life in a positive way:

_____

_____

_____

Now, think about what specific qualities they exhibit that you particularly like. Perhaps you like the way they seem to care about you and how they take the time to listen to you. These people always seem to offer just the right words and advice at the right time. If they are people whom you don't know but admire from afar, how can you emulate their values and traits? Your ideal self is the part of you that represents the highest level of achievement and behavior in your life. If you constantly move in that direction, you will always be on the right path.

Your *self-image* is the perception you have about you when you think about yourself. When you look into a mirror, do you like the person who looks back at you? Most people would like to change some aspects about themselves when they look at their body. Your body, however, is just a very small part of who you are. It is the physical part of you that you present to the world. However, it is not the entire you. You can make some alterations to your body by diet and exercise, but in the long run, try to like your body and accept the style, make, and model that has been given you.

Your *self-esteem* is not your body but how you feel about yourself. Are you a good person? Do other people like being around you? Do you make a positive impact on other people? People feel good about who they are to the degree that they respect who they are. Most feelings of low self-esteem come from negative past experiences. If influential people in your life made you feel inadequate as a child, and the criticism continued for years, you will likely have doubts about yourself as you grow older. People tend to accept other people's beliefs about them, regardless of the facts, especially if those people are parents, teachers, and bosses. No matter what happened to you in the past, you can change your opinion of yourself.

Self-improvement begins with a willingness to learn and grow. Start by considering the following:

• *Examine the values and principles by which you live.* A value is a behavior trait that you think is important. Good values include things like being honest, trustworthy, and hard working. What behavioral traits do you value? If you're not sure, think of someone you admire. What are some of their values?

• *Learn from your mistakes.* We grow by making mistakes and learning from them. Don't be afraid to make mistakes. Ralph Waldo Emerson said, "Men succeed when they realize that their failures are the preparation for their victories." If you think about it, weren't the times of greatest learning in your life the times when you made the biggest mistakes? As painful as it sometimes is in the short term, making mistakes can help you learn more in the long term.

• *Choose positive influences.* Successful people surround themselves with others who have a positive influence on their lives. There's an old saying that goes, "It's hard to soar with the eagles when you scratch with the turkeys." Don't waste time being around people who are constantly negative. Be friendly, but make a 180-degree turn and move away from them. Negativity is a nasty and infectious disease. You don't want to be anywhere near it.

• **_Respect yourself._** It's hard to get others to respect you if you don't respect yourself. No matter what happened in the past, you can take steps to improve how you feel about yourself starting today. You are not a collection of what others think of you. You can't control other people, but you can control how you react to other people. Eleanor Roosevelt said, "No one can make you feel inferior without your consent." Make a commitment to improve how you feel about yourself. It's never too late to start.

You are what you think about. James Allen, an Englishman who lived from 1864 to 1912, said, "As a man thinketh in his heart so is he." How you think about yourself, to a large degree, will determine how successful you will be in your life. Your character will become the sum total of all your thoughts. Outstanding achievers are ordinary people who have learned to overcome the negative programming that has occurred in the past. Self-improvement starts with the thoughts you have about yourself.

The next time you find yourself being down or depressed, consider the following people who overcame overwhelming adversity and achieved greatness.

• Ludwig van Beethoven (1770-1827) lost his hearing by age 46. Yet, he wrote his greatest music during his later years.

• Louis Braille (1809-1852) was blinded at age three. He became a teacher in Paris and later developed the Braille system.

• Helen Keller (1880-1968) was blind and deaf by age two, yet she wrote 10 books and is loved by millions.

• Franklin D. Roosevelt (1882-1945) taught Americans that "The only thing we have to fear, is fear itself," during the height of the Great Depression. He was paralyzed by polio at age 39 but is known as one of America's greatest presidents.

• Wilma Rudolf (1940-1994) overcame childhood ailments including polio, pneumonia and scarlet fever, which some said would prevent her from ever walking. During the Olympic Games in Rome in 1960, she went on to win three gold metals in the 100-meter dash, the 200-meter dash, and the 400-meter relay. In 1993, she became the first recipient of President Clinton's National Sports Award.

Do you think Christopher Reeve will ever walk again? He does.

The MOTHER Model

Your thoughts are the starting point for maximizing your potential. Programming yourself for success is the key to reaching that potential, and it doesn't have to be hard. Consider this model:

Thoughts ⟶ Feelings ⟶ Actions = Results

How you think determines how you feel; how you feel determines your actions; and your actions determine the results in your life. The ability to choose your thoughts is the starting point for getting the results you want in your life. These thoughts, when combined with action, will help you reach your potential.

To help you understand how thoughts, feelings and actions come together and make up who you are, I created the MOTHER model. MOTHER is an acronym that stands for *Moments of Truth Have Everlasting Repercussions*. Basically, this means that every time you interact with another human being, that is a moment of truth. What you say and how you act can and will have everlasting consequences or repercussions. This "moment of truth" helps create your relationship with others. Therefore, try to make every interaction with another person a good one, regardless of the circumstance or situation. Doing that will help you make a significant, positive difference in their lives.

Your conscious mind is the part of you that chooses thoughts or makes choices. The subconscious mind is the part of you that makes up your feelings. Your body is the vehicle that helps you put your thoughts and feelings into motion. Your spirit is your sensitive, directive force. The whole of you is more than the sum of these parts.

Programming Your Subconscious

There are basically four ways to program your subconscious. Remember, everything that you experience in your life, is registered in your subconscious mind, and much of it you can influence. You can program your subconscious mind in a positive way through repetition, significant emotional events, first impressions, and bizarre events.

- **Repetition** is the method used by your grade school teacher when she taught you the multiplication tables. She made you repeat it over and over again, until the answers were ingrained in your head. Companies who advertise on television figure that if the viewing public sees the commercial enough times, they'll be more likely to buy the product.

- **Significant emotional events** are events that happen in your life that "stop you in your tracks" and make you take notice. These events make a huge difference in your life. Where were you when you heard the news on September 11, 2001? The events at the World Trade Center and the Pentagon will be remembered by people all over the world. These events can also have a positive impact on your life as well. Do you know anyone who has won the lottery? I bet he or she remembers that event too!

- **First impressions** are first events that happen to you. For example, do you remember your first visit to Disney World, the first time in an airplane, your first day on the job with your current employer, or your first sexual experience? I'll bet you do. Most first impressions, whether they are positive or negative, are usually remembered forever.

- **Bizarre events** are those unexpected, out-of-the-ordinary happenings and coincidences. For example, have you ever been on vacation, only to see someone whom you didn't expect to see, perhaps someone you work with? Seeing this person out of the normal context is a bit bizarre. You remember it because this experience is unexpected.

Most of the news on television is negative—a tragic accident, a shooting, someone getting robbed, a house burning down. Roughly 80 percent of television news is negative, 10 percent is positive, and 10 percent is neutral. If you're not careful, this constant bombardment of negative news can have a negative impact on your disposition. Be careful to balance what you watch on television. Many shows deliver a positive message.

In her book *Why is Everyone So Cranky?*, C. Leslie Charles says, "We're a nation whose collective mood has gone sour. On our streets and highways, in our workplaces, and even in our homes, we've abandoned common courtesy."

Goal-oriented people generally don't like to be around negative people. If you always see the negative side, people will not want to be around you. This negative outlook will hurt your career, even if you are a top performer. So don't get caught up in a negative cycle. Acknowledge negative people, but do not spend any time with them. Try to be around positive people. The people with whom you associate play a big part on how you are perceived at work.

Can you think of individuals at work whom most people think are jerks but the company tolerates them because they get results? Every company has one or two of these people. Companies usually keep these people in their jobs because they get results. However, these people are likely to be plateaued in their careers because of their bad attitudes. Keeping these people in place causes morale problems within the company. One bad apple really can spoil the whole bunch. In the long run, companies lose productivity by tolerating negative behavior. Get around positive people and stay there.

How's Your "Self-Talk?"

Self-talk can be defined as the chatter that goes on inside your head on a daily basis. What kind of comments do you say to yourself, about yourself? These thoughts have a tremendous influence on your performance. Consider the following negative thoughts, Have you ever said any of them to yourself?

It won't work.	I hate Mondays.
It's not my fault.	It's not my job.
They don't work hard.	I'm stupid.
I'm tired.	I'm overworked and underpaid.
My job is not important.	Nobody tells me anything.
What's the use?	There's no money in the budget.
I've never done that before.	Been there, done that.
I told you so.	My job is going nowhere.
I don't have any patience.	I can't remember names.
They'll probably say no.	It's their fault.
Traffic is awful.	People drive like maniacs.
It figures it would rain today.	I hate vegetables.
My taxes are too high.	Life's hard, and then you die.
My boss won't listen to me.	I'll never amount to anything.

Negative thinking can lead to negative statements. Making negative statements causes the subconscious to process that information as being real. The subconscious mind does not know the difference between real or simulated experiences—it only knows what you said and believes it to be true. These statements, said over and over again, will lead you to believe the statement, whether it is true or not. Over time, you may start to believe the comments that other people say about you. Many times these statements are far from the truth.

Self-talk is something that you can control. In a society where we are constantly being told what to do, what to say, how to look, how to feel, how to act and what to wear, it sure is comforting to know that we can still control our thoughts. You may not be able to control the things that happen to you, but you can control how you think about the things that happen to you. Since choosing your thoughts is something that you control, choose wisely.

When programming your subconscious, use a positive affirmation—a statement that is both positive and is stated in the present tense. Affirmations begin with "I am, I have, I can." Consider the following statements:

"I am good at remembering other people's names."
"I am a healthy person."
"I have a lot of patience."
"I have what it takes to succeed."
"I can make a difference."
"I can do it."

These statements, repeated over and over again, will program your subconscious mind for success. Combine these statements with a dash of confidence and make good things happen in your life. There's a difference between positive thinking and positive knowing. If you believe in a positive outcome, it just might happen. However, if you believe in a negative outcome, negative results are sure to happen. The power of positive expectations, *believing in yourself,* must be the cornerstone of your code of conduct if you are serious about making a difference in this world.

Your body is the physical part of you that other people see—the part of you that you present to the world. Do people judge you by your outward appearance? Yes, they do. Can those judgements be unfair? Yes, they can. Be who you want to be; however, know that other people will be constantly judging you. You have 100 percent control over the clothes you wear. Always try to look your best. You never know whom you might come in contact with. Be your best, and look your best.

Here are a few common names for the law of nature:
- Cause and effect
- Garbage in, garbage out
- Sowing and reaping
- Action, reaction
- What goes around, comes around

The law of nature says that whatever you do (cause) will have a consequence (effect) which will be either positive, negative, or neutral. Nothing exists in a vacuum. Everything you do or don't do, say or don't say, has a consequence. You can control the outcome of events more than you think. Henry Ford said, "If you think you can or if you think you can't, you're right." Improving your attitude will make an amazing difference in your life.

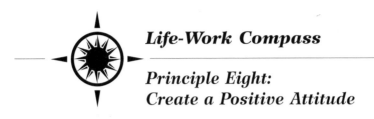

Life-Work Compass

Principle Eight:
Create a Positive Attitude

What?
1. Eliminate the entitlement mentality.
2. Reciprocate kindness.
3. Successful people have positive attitudes.
4. Program your subconscious mind positively.
5. Create positive self-talk.

Why?
1. Because no one owes you anything.
2. Because that's what successful people do.
3. Because attitude and success are intertwined.
4. To realize positive expectations.
5. To program yourself for success.

How?
1. By not keeping score of who does what.
2. By looking for ways to initiate or return favors.
3. By looking at the positive rather than the negative.
4. By using positive affirmations (I can, I am, I have).
5. By always being a cheerleader for yourself.

When?
1. Starting from this day forward.
2. Anytime you see an opportunity.
3. Anytime you are faced with a difficult challenge.
4. Starting today.
5. Anytime you are faced with a difficult challenge.

Be Playful

Putting Joy Back into the Workplace

How do you balance your work life and your personal life? Separating your job from your personal life can be a very difficult. Finding the right balance can mean the difference between having joy in your life and living a life of drudgery.

Adding joy to your life is one way to create happiness and peace of mind. Joy is evoked by well-being, success, good fortune, or by the prospect of possessing what you desire. Clearly defining what you desire and then creating a plan for achieving those desires can evoke a feeling of well-being. Having a good sense of humor is one way to lighten your load and reduce stress while trying to achieve a balanced life. We all need to laugh more often.

On a scale of 1 to 10, with 10 being high, how would you rate how satisfied are you in your job right now? If you find your answer is below 5, you need to look at ways to add joy back into your work and make your work more rewarding and fulfilling. Going to a job every day that you hate will suck the life right out of you.

There's no guarantee that you will be happy all the time. On the other hand, you need not live a life of despair either. Thomas Jefferson suggested that people have the right to pursue happiness when he wrote: "We hold these truths to be self-evident, that all men are created equal, that they are endowed by their Creator with certain unalienable Rights, that among these are Life, Liberty and the pursuit of Happiness."

We all have the right to pursue happiness in our lives. All of us, however, define happiness in our own terms. What makes one person happy will not necessarily make another person happy. We are all unique in what makes our lives personally fulfilling. We all need to identify what makes us happy and then move in that direction.

Paradoxically, it is only through being sad that we know happiness. Without sadness, we would not know happiness. Without darkness, we would not know light. Without evil, we would not know goodness. This law of opposites provides us with the opportunity to choose the path we take in our lives. We can choose to pursue happiness, or we can choose despair. By deciding not to choose at all, we become victims of circumstances. Happiness should be a lifelong pursuit that takes into account periods of unhappiness. The unhappy periods, however, are just as important to our learning and growth. Benjamin Franklin said, "Those things that hurt, instruct." All of us experience tough times, and through those tough times we have an opportunity to become stronger. There's an old saying that goes, "Things that don't kill you make you stronger." Tough times should not be looked upon as bad times. Sometimes, the bad experience helps to wake you up. Some people sleepwalk through their lives. Sleepwalking is the same as idling in neutral—there is no forward movement. If you are currently experiencing a difficult stretch in your life, look upon it as a way to help you discover who you are. Circumstances do not make us who we are; they simply reveal us to ourselves. Life's challenges teach us valuable lessons. Welcome challenge as an opportunity to grow.

An occasional difficult situation is different from a chronic bad situation. Some people have had the same job for years, even though they hate it. Are they so frozen with fear that it causes them to be immobile? Hopefully, you don't fall into this category. Life is too short to spend it working in a job that you hate. Not only is this unhealthy for you, it's unhealthy for people who work with you. Sometimes, you can be the right person but in the wrong job. Wise are those who know when a job is not right for them, and then do something about it.

Successful people often either create the jobs they want or do things to make the job a more comfortable fit. Deciding to do nothing is not a good choice. You don't always have to be promoted. Sometimes a lateral transfer might do the trick. Choosing the correct job for you will help create joy, not only in the workplace but in your personal life as well. Only you can determine the correct path. Robert Frost said it best in his timeless poem, *Road Less Traveled.*

Two roads diverged in a yellow wood
And sorry I could not travel both
And be one traveler, long I stood
And looked down one as far as I could
To where it bent in the undergrowth

Then took the other as just as fair
And having perhaps the better claim
Because it was grassy and wanted wear
Though as for that, the passing there
Had worn them really about the same

And both that morning equally lay
In leaves no step had trodden black
Oh, I kept the first for another day!
Yet, knowing how way leads onto way
I doubted if I should ever come back

I shall be telling this with a sigh
Somewhere ages and ages hence
Two roads diverged in a wood
And I took the one less traveled by
And that has made all the difference

Since every person is unique, try not to judge the chosen path of others. Singer and song writer, Jackson Browne said, "People take different roads seeking fulfillment and happiness. Just because they are not on your road does not mean they are lost." Choose the right path for you, and honor the path chosen by others. Answering two questions may help you choose the right path:

- What do you enjoy doing?
- What are you very good at doing?

The answers can help point you in the right direction. The points on a compass represent all possible directions. You, however, must choose the direction that feels right for you—and that's the best direction of all. If you know that you're headed in the right direction, all you have to do is keep moving forward.

Once you have identified the things that you like and you're good at doing, set a deadline for when you'd like to begin moving in that direction. There's nothing like having a deadline to motivate yourself. Research your interests. Identify people who have already done what you would like to do. Interview them, and ask them how they did it. Many successful people would love to tell you about their experience—learn from them!

Make the Most of Your Job

Did you ever notice people who seem to love their jobs? When you watch them go about their routine, it doesn't even seem that they are working. In fact, it seems that they are playing rather than working. They have jobs that are challenging, rewarding, and fun. Some people are lucky enough to find jobs that they love. Other people create the jobs they love. Either way, successful people make the most of their careers. They don't rely on others to make their career for them.

To have more joy in the workplace, begin by not taking yourself too seriously. Author, John Andrew Holmes said, "It is well to remember that the entire population of the universe, with one trifling exception, is composed of others." As important as you think your job is, if it were eliminated tomorrow, chances are the company would not go out of business. People who work hard but still enjoy their jobs seem to be on a mission. They are filled with life and a sense of purpose. Successful people create their own purpose and then add enthusiasm to get results. Abraham Lincoln once said,

"In the end, it's not the years in your life that count. It's the life in your years." Life is too short to spend it complaining about things you don't like in your job. Lighten up and enjoy the ride. You'll feel better, and you'll be a better person for it.

Take full advantage of the opportunities for advancement that your job affords you. Once, I had a job at a utility company where I held the title of Junior Engineer. After I completed a series of tests on a variety of subjects and gained a certain amount of seniority, I qualified for a promotion to an Associate Engineer. This level offered more money and more perks. As I look back on that experience, I realize that I had a lot of fun "pursuing" the next level.

Are you currently working toward the next level of your job, or have you settled for your current level? Are you happy where you are? Some people are perfectly content with staying in their current jobs. There is nothing wrong with that, as long as they choose to stay there. If you are not content and have opportunity to reach the next level, you may wish to take steps and move in that direction. Doing so can create purpose in your career, which can then add joy to your job. Reaching the next level in your job might open doors that have been previously closed to you. What do you have to lose?

What's Your Purpose?

Being joyful at work has nothing to do with the activities or functions you perform, but has everything to do with purpose. What is your purpose at work? Why do you work? Making money is important and certainly a good reason to work, but it does not necessarily define your purpose at work or, for that matter, your purpose in life. Purpose can be defined as your reason for getting up in the morning. A person without purpose is like a ship without a rudder, drifting aimlessly in the ocean of life. A person without purpose can easily get knocked off course. A person with purpose, however, is always moving in the direction of his or her dreams. You acquire joy along the way by reaching the benchmarks that you set for yourself.

Self-Assessment

Following are three very important questions for you to answer. The answers to these three questions will help you determine your purpose at work.

What is the mission of your company? _____

_____

_____

Why does your team or department exist? _____

_____

_____

Why are you on the payroll? _____

_____

_____

As you look at the answers to these questions, do you list making money as the primary answer? It's okay if you do because making money certainly is important. Making money is a good thing. People who don't understand money claim it's the root of all evil. I disagree. It's how you use money that's important. Many people just don't have a good understanding of the value of money. It is simply a tool that will help you accomplish or acquire the things you desire. What you wish to accomplish is up to you.

So how do you make money? I maintain that if a company goes into business to make money, it will fail. However, if a company goes into business to create, serve, and satisfy customers—the money will follow. Serving the customer now becomes your purpose at work. Joy comes from fulfilling this purpose. Being in the service of others is one of the highest purposes for working.

Have you found where you "fit" best in the workplace? Consider yourself one piece of a 1,000-piece puzzle. The puzzle represents your company, and you represent one piece of the puzzle. Does your piece fit nicely into the puzzle, or have you forced it into place? Some poor souls don't know where they fit. It's a great feeling to know that you have found the exact space where your puzzle piece fits. However, you may outgrow your puzzle and need to move on to more difficult challenges as they present themselves.

For example, you may have exhausted all the opportunity in your present position with your company. If your job is no longer challenging, perhaps it is time to move on. Consider a lateral transfer to another department. You don't always need to be promoted up the chain of command. Sometimes, just a change of scenery is all it takes for you to "bloom." Sometimes, you can go into a position with much trepidation and discover you really like it. Try not to discount something before you have a chance to learn whether you'll like it or not. Doing "due diligence" is a mark of successful people. Investigate and research new opportunities.

The following list of things that can contribute to a good working environment may give you some ideas for making a course correction in your career. The more things you check, the greater the satisfaction in your job.

____ My job is challenging but not overwhelming.
____ There is opportunity for advancement.
____ I feel good that I'm accomplishing something important.
____ I am recognized and rewarded for my work.
____ I feel that I am part of the organization.
____ I make a significant contribution.
____ Customers interact with me and give me positive feedback.
____ I am paid well for the work I perform.
____ Company benefits are in line with the competition.
____ I enjoy my coworkers (for the most part).
____ My boss communicates with me regularly.
____ I feel "in" on things.
____ My input is sought on a regular basis.
____ People tease me (in a nice way).
____ I am asked to be a part of challenging projects.
____ I am put on select committees.
____ I am asked to report on things at meetings.

    ____ My boss allows me to have flextime.
    ____ There is variety in my daily work.
    ____ Goals are in place and clearly understood.
    ____ I get excited about upcoming events.
    ____ I feel that I belong to something bigger than myself.
    ____ My workspace is located so that I feel part of the action.
    ____ I have promotion opportunities.
    ____ Money is available for training, and I am paid to attend.
    ____ I enjoy my job.

                ____Total number of checkmarks

20 to 26	Congratulations, you have found your niche.
15 to 19	You're comfortable for now but seek opportunity.
10 to 14	Maybe you should update your resume.
6 to 9	You definitely should update your resume.
5 or below	Get another job soon.

If you didn't score high on this test, the "joy factor" in your current job is not what it could be. You need to decide if you want to start searching for a new job. You should exhaust all possible jobs within your company before you look elsewhere. There's nothing wrong with talking to your boss and letting him or her know that you would like to be promoted or transferred. You need to schedule a meeting with your boss and discuss possible career opportunities. This conversation should occur outside of the office if possible, perhaps during lunch. No one needs to know about your intentions.

Creating More Options in Your Job

If you have a job that is sucking the life out of you, you must quit before it starts to affect your health. I see too many people who just go through the motions in their jobs, putting in their time to collect a paycheck. These people are retired in place.

Your job doesn't have to be exciting every minute of every day; but hopefully, there are more up days than down days. If you really hate your job, do yourself a favor and quit. Your friends, family, and employer deserve more from you. The following items will provide you with more options in your career:

• *If you don't have a college degree, get one.* If your company has a tuition reimbursement policy, take advantage of it. That money has been allocated for employee use. Even if your company just pays a partial amount, accept it graciously. Investigate the colleges around where you live. Find out what they have to offer and how their curriculum fits into your life's purpose.

• *If you don't have an advanced degree, get one.* If you already have an undergraduate degree, consider an advanced degree. A Master's degree takes only two more years. Your thesis can be written about something you are working on in your job.

• *Volunteer for company projects.* This is one of the quickest ways to show your boss that you are a team player. It is also a great way to learn new and interesting things about your company and its customers.

• *Learn as much about your company as possible.* Know as much about your company as possible, not just what's going on in your department. Read everything that your company publishes. If your company has a library, visit it often and check out the available material.

• *Be around the right people.* The people who get ahead are the ones who move through difficult tasks and don't spend time whining. It's more fun being around people who look at the positive things in life.

• *Know why you are on the payroll.* Knowing this will foster a sense of duty and responsibility. Serving your customer to the best of your ability will give you a sense of accomplishment.

• *Don't take yourself too seriously.* Life is too short to be so serious all the time. Enjoy life and be able to laugh at yourself. When things get a little tough, try to keep them in perspective. Dr. Robert Schuler said, "Tough times don't last, but tough people do."

• *Avoid multi-tasking everything.* Every minute of every day does not have to be spent doing something. Relax once in a while. Quiet time has a lot of value.

• *Don't take your work home every night.* Your time at home is a time to unwind and get away from work. Try not to spend all evening talking about what happened at work that day. The burnout factor speeds up when all you talk about is work. Besides that, you become boring to those around you. If all you do is talk about your work, you might find your family and friends trying to avoid you.

• *If you work indoors, spend time outdoors.* Get some fresh air. Take a walk around the block or in a park or mountain. Mother Nature has a unique way of regenerating us. It's also good for your health to exercise outdoors once in a while.

• *Get enough sleep.* Not having enough sleep will have a negative effect on you in your job. You know how much sleep your body needs—make sure you get it! If you need to cut back on something, make sure it's not your sleep time. It's no fun working when you're exhausted.

• *When you're sick, stay home.* Nobody admires someone who is sick but comes to work and infects everyone else. Do yourself and others a big favor when you're sick: Stay home—your body is trying to tell you something.

• *Look for the positive side of people and things.* Things happen for a reason. Try to learn something from everything that happens to you in your life. No person's mission in life is to make you miserable—you tend to do that to yourself. Try to learn from every person and event in your life.

• *Take necessary breaks.* When you push yourself too hard for too long, quality will start to drop. Taking five-minute breaks here and there is good for your spirit. Stretch your legs and refresh your mind. Try to get out of the office for lunch. Leaving the building and then returning after lunch can give you just the spark you need.

• *Create a positive office space.* Try to surround yourself with things that make you feel good—things like pictures of important people, reminders of past accomplishments, and colorful artwork. Remember, this is where you spend your time away from home—make it warm and personal.

Creating More Options in Your Life

The following suggestions will help you balance your personal life:

• *Find a hobby or leisure activity.* When you get home, do something that you enjoy doing—something completely different from the things that you do at work.

• ***Reconnect with your family.*** Most people say that their family is the most important thing in their lives, but they don't behave accordingly. When given the choice between demands at work and needs at home, most people sacrifice the needs of their family. Be there for the important things in your kids' lives. Those times never come around again.

• ***Take care of yourself.*** Your body will tell you when something is wrong. Headaches, upset stomach, and body aches and pains are symptoms that you are overdoing it. Listen to your body and what it's telling you. Pushing forward without watching the warning signs is dangerous.

• ***Drive the speed limit.*** Traffic in some cities is a nightmare. Road construction is everywhere. One thing that you might try when you are driving is to slow down and drive the speed limit rather than fight traffic. Leave a little earlier and take your time. Change your mindset and welcome cars that are trying to merge into traffic.

• ***Minimize social obligations.*** Belonging to social organizations can take up large amounts of your time, especially if you are an officer or board member. Religious obligations take time as well. Join and participate in organizations that give you the most value.

• ***Don't waste time worrying.*** Worrying about things consumes your energy. Being overly concerned about future events can cause mental distress. Controlling your fear is the first step in reducing your worry time.

• ***Don't live by other people's standards.*** Trying to live up to other people's standards and expectations is difficult. You won't please some people, no matter what you do. Those people love telling you what you do wrong, and they tell you every chance they get. Try living to the beat of your own drum.

• ***Learn to let go of the past.*** Things that happened to you in the past have a way of sticking with you your entire life. Those "anchors" are dead weight that prevent you from moving forward. Give yourself permission to leave all that baggage behind.

• ***Stop trying to be perfect.*** No one is perfect. Everyone makes mistakes. It takes entirely too much energy to constantly try to be perfect. You have more important things to do than keep track of your mistakes.

• ***Be playful.*** Take some time to watch a toddler play. Better yet, if you have a toddler in the family, go out in the back yard and play with him or her. If you've forgotten how to play, I'm sure the child will show you. Don't forget to bring your imagination.

• ***Try to keep things in perspective.*** Nothing is ever as bad as it seems or as good as it looks. Be flexible enough to deal with whatever comes your way. Finding purpose in your life can be a lifelong endeavor, but a calm mind and a peaceful heart come from knowing who you are. Learn to be comfortable with who you are.

In his book, *As a Man Thinketh*, James Allen said, "How many we know who sour their lives, who ruin all that is sweet and beautiful by explosive tempers, who destroy their poise of character, and make bad blood! It is a question whether the great majority of people do not ruin their lives and mar their happiness by lack of self control. How few people we meet in life who are well-balanced, who have that exquisite poise which is characteristic of the finished character!" Be playful, add joy to your life, and seek balance.

Managing Stress

Everyone feels stress. Trying to eliminate stress from our lives is not only impractical, it's unhealthy. Each of us must learn to live with stress because there's no such thing as a stress-free environment. Stress is simply the extra pressure that we make on our mind and body. People respond differently to stress. When does the stress become too much? Why are some people at greater risk than others? Why do some people panic in an emergency while others seem to think clearly?

It's not the amount of stress in your life but how you react to stress that will determine your success. Effectively managing stress is a key to reaching your potential. Knowing the warning signs of stress and then managing that stress will help you navigate through some difficult times in your life. Here are some ways your body will show signs of stress:

• Headache, chest pain, dizziness, weakness
• Upset stomach, hiccoughs, diarrhea

- Tightness or twitching of muscles
- Frequent minor pain
- Nail biting
- Changes in sleeping habits
- Constant tiredness or irritability
- Problems concentrating

The long-term effects of stress can affect the body in negative ways. When your body is under constant stress, it is less able to fight off illness or disease. The longer you suffer from a stressful situation, the greater your chances of becoming sick. Stress should not be confused with tension. Tension is similar to stretching a rubber band. The greater the stretch, the more stress it produces. Tension leads to stress. Constant tension will create stress and strain on your body. Here are some causes of stress in life and job situations.

Life Situations	Job Situations
Death of a spouse	Deadlines
Divorce	Unclear goals
Marital separation	Abrasive boss
Jail term	Lack of leadership
Death of a family member	Low salary
Personal injury or illness	Threat of being fired
Marriage	Incompetent co-workers
Loss of job	Technology changes
Retirement	Too many meetings
Pregnancy	Boredom in job
New baby	Lack of resources
Major change in income	Lack of privacy
Taking out a mortgage or loan	Conflicting demands
Son or daughter leaving home	Unclear authority
Trouble with in-laws	Mistrust of those in power
Spouse begins or stops work	Office politics
Trouble with your boss	Sarcastic remarks
Change in residence	Sexual harassment
Holidays	Rude people
Violation of the law	Whiners

The best way to reduce stress is to create some effective coping strategies. Here are some coping strategies that you might consider:

- *Get things out in the open.* Express your feelings and emotions. Keeping them bottled up is not good. Open communication is essential for good stress management.
- *Schedule downtime.* Take some time for yourself. Everyone needs a break to regenerate the batteries.
- *Engage in physical activity.* Exercising has a way of purging your body of unwanted stress.
- *Learn to say "no."* Never feel obligated to do something that you don't want to do. Not being able to say "no" can lead to resentment and stress.
- *Manage your time.* Read Chapter 5.

There is good in every situation. Even bad situations have a way of teaching us new things about ourselves. If you look for the good in people, you will find it. You are the master of your own destiny. Life is too short not to be happy. Putting joy back into your personal life and professional career will help you takes steps in the right direction.

Life-Work Compass

Principle Nine:
Be Playful

What?
1. Choose a path in life that feels right for you.
2. If you really hate your job, you must quit.
3. Not all things that hurt in your life are bad.
4. Try to make the most of your job.
5. Keep things in perspective.

Why?
1. If you don't, life will choose it for you.
2. If you don't, it will suck the life out of you.
3. Because they can teach you valuable lessons.
4. Because it is where you spend a good deal of your life.
5. Because nothing is ever as bad as it seems.

How?
1. By identifying what you like and what you're good at doing.
2. By creating a deadline for yourself.
3. By helping you identify what to move away from.
4. By seeking opportunity.
5. By balancing the bad with the good.

When?
1. Anytime you find yourself at a crossroad in life.
2. When you have a job that is not right for you.
3. When things don't go your way.
4. Throughout the year.
5. Anytime something bad happens.

Be Service Oriented

The State of Customer Service Today

If you're like most people, you've probably had a bad experience doing business with another company sometime in your life. If that incident was particularly bad, you probably still remember it in vivid detail. In fact, if you think about the incident, you can perhaps even recall the emotions you felt at the time.

There's no doubt that customer service needs some improvement. In his book *Customer Love*, Chip R. Bell says, "Customers are less patient, more finicky, less trusting, and more astute regarding the worth of service." People are in a hurry these days and don't have time to deal with a company that doesn't understand the value of exceptional customer service.

I hope that the following list of customer service flaws gives you some ideas for improving your customer service.

Telephone Use:

• *Automated telephone greetings.* Companies use automated telephone greetings to save money; however, don't you feel you deserve to have a live person answer the phone—or at least have the option to talk to a live person? Pressing a series of numbers to try to get through to the person to whom you wish to speak seems hostile. If a company is trying to establish a friendly relationship with their customers, then using an automated greeting isn't the way to do it. There's no substitute for a live person.

If your phone system has this feature, there's not much you can do about it except to work within the system. If a customer is trying to contact you after going through an automated greeting, try to personally answer your phone. It's very frustrating to finally get through to the right person only to get another automated message. Greet the caller with a warm "hello" and a sincere desire to help.

My wife recently told me of an experience she had with our local telephone company. Telephone companies don't have the best reputation for good customer service. However, when my wife called the telephone company to inquire about our current billing rate, she was greeted by a young woman who said, "Hello, I'm Sarah, and I'm going to give you exceptional customer service." This greeting is very smart because it makes the individual answering the phone personally responsible and establishes an expectation for the call. Being somewhat skeptical, my wife proceeded reluctantly with the call. But in the end, she was provided a money-saving rate. The experience was such a pleasant surprise that my wife had to tell me about it—and now I'm telling you. Wouldn't it be great if all customer calls ended that way?

• *Voice mail.* I have voice mail on my business and personal telephones. I think it's a good feature if used properly. However, what's annoying is when people hide behind their voice mail in an attempt to eliminate the telephone from interrupting them from other, more "important" matters. What could be more important than serving your customer? Your customers are the lifeblood to your organization. Used properly, voice mail is a good tool, but don't have it engaged all day long.

Some people change their voice mail message daily. If you have this option and aren't currently taking advantage of it, you may want to consider it. Personally, I appreciate when I am informed that the person whom I am calling is out of the office for three days. Now I have the option to leave a message on their phone or wait until they return. Leaving an updated message indicates that this person cares about their callers. Try to change your message when you know you will be gone from your job for an extended period of time. This sends a message to your callers that you care about them.

• ***People who don't return phone messages.*** I think it is very rude when the person whom I'm calling with a legitimate question does not return my call. I know I may not be the most important thing on that person's "to do" list; however, it's common courtesy to acknowledge your callers. If you're using voice mail, the least you could do is return your messages! You can easily impress your callers by recognizing their call and getting back to them in a timely manner. No one is too important not to return phone calls. Not returning your calls will tarnish your image as a good provider of customer service.

• ***Transfers.*** Few people today want to deal with the caller if the caller's request does not directly affect them. Personally, when I get transferred several times, I feel like I have some sort of disease. If you take a call and the customer explains that they have already been transferred several times, tell the customer that you will personally call the right person and have them get back to you. How refreshing! Remember, the telephone is not an interruption of your day. When that phone rings, think of it as your job calling you.

• ***Long-winded messages.*** There's nothing more irritating than when callers leave a long-winded message and then tell you their phone number so fast that you don't have time to write it down. Now, you have to listen to that annoying message again just to hear the phone number repeated. When you leave your phone number on voice mail, speak slowly! You might state your name and phone number at both the beginning and at the end of your message. This gives the other person two opportunities to hear the information correctly.

Regarding retail stores, airlines, and hotels:

• ***Finding someone to wait on you.*** Don't you hate having to track someone down in a department store so you can ask a question or make a purchase? In an effort to save some money, companies eliminate a very important person in the store—the sales associate. Doing this will save the store money in the short term, but they will lose money in the long term. When people learn that there is no one to wait on them, they will choose to go to another store that values customer service.

Think about some of the big department stores in your local mall. Assuming that the price and the quality of the products are competitive, which store do you prefer? You'll choose the store that you know has friendly people who are willing to wait on you. The store that provides good customer service will create market share. Customer service pays.

• *Getting punished at check-out time.* Isn't it annoying to wait in a long line to pay for your purchase? Isn't there a manager somewhere watching the long line of customers and making more cashiers available to wait on the people standing in line? Companies should be eager to take your money, not punish you at the end of your experience with their store.

Over time, I log a fair amount of air miles in my training and consulting job. I am a frequent flyer with more than one airline. There is one airline, however, that I dread flying due to the extremely long lines at check-in. I know that security has been tightened lately; however, those long lines were there long before September 11, 2001. I try to stay away from that particular airline. They constantly overbook their flights and have, in my opinion, the most "weather-related" delays in the industry. My time is important to me, and having to wait in long lines at department stores or at the airport will definitely make me think about choosing another store or airline. It all comes down to customer service.

• *Inconsistent airfares.* Many airlines are hurting today. However, it shouldn't take a national disaster to lower airfares. Being a frequent flyer, I've never understood how prices can fluctuate so much within the same airline, let alone between other airlines. The airfare shouldn't depend on whether you come back on Friday or Saturday. It's obvious that supply-and-demand economics are a factor here, however, it's mind boggling that the airline industry has such a wide fluctuation in prices. Can you imagine your company charging a certain price for its product or service depending on the day of the week? Prices are important to the buying customer. Find out why your company prices its products or services the way it does and take the time to inform your customers.

• *Quoting company policy.* Company policies are designed to protect the company, not to help the consumer. A person should not have to go through the third degree when returning an item to the store. If you paid cash, not a check for the item, then you should receive cash back—immediately! Having to wait two weeks for a check to be issued to you from the store's corporate headquarters because it's "company policy" protects the store, not you.

Of course, you have to follow the policy and standards that your company has in place; otherwise, you will get into trouble. But don't hide behind your company's policy as the sole reason why you can't serve the customer. There are ways to satisfy the customer's request while not breaking company policy. It is very annoying to have a sales clerk inform me of all the things that can't be done. I want to know what can be done. I try to focus on the positives rather than the negatives. You want to be known in your company as a problem solver rather than a problem giver.

• *Hotel reservations.* I've often wondered why a hotel has such difficulty confirming your room at the time you make the reservation. How many times have you heard, "I'll put down that you prefer a non-smoking room; however, I can't guarantee it until you check in." Why? Don't hotels have computers? I've never worked in the hotel business, but confirming a nonsmoking room shouldn't be so hard.

Las Vegas is not particularly known for its great customer service. Again, supply-and-demand economics indicate that perhaps they don't need to provide good customer service due to the hundreds of thousands of people who go there each year. Many hotels have the "too bad, so what" philosophy. However, in the months following September 11, 2001, many people were reluctant to travel. Isn't it interesting that we're now seeing more commercials from Las Vegas and the airlines.

Successful companies, and the people who work in those companies, value good customer service. They create a "How may I serve you philosophy." And, this philosophy is consistent throughout the year, not just during slow times.

Serving others is a wonderful opportunity to show people who you are. You provide the highest levels of service by becoming more interested in other people's wants and needs rather than your own.

How to Distinguish Yourself

There are basically three ways a company can differentiate itself from the competition: 1) price, 2) quality and 3) service. The greatest of these, in my opinion, is service. When you look at your company's competitors, they probably offer a similar product or service at a competitive price. Also, their product or service may be of comparable quality to what your company offers. You naturally think that your company is better, but there's probably not much difference in quality and price between your company and other companies. How a company really makes an impact on its customers is by providing excellent customer service. This is where a company can run circles around the competition and increase its share of the market.

When you hear the name of a particular company, do you have an impression of that company? That impression, real or imagined, is what makes up that company's image. So too, when your name is mentioned in your company, others have an impression of you too. You want to do everything possible to have people to think of you in a positive manner. You want to earn a reputation as someone who can get things done and can be trusted. You want to be thought of as someone who provides outstanding customer service day in and day out.

Your reputation, productivity, and image will help you reach the level you seek in your organization. One of the best ways to distinguish yourself in your organization is to consider everyone you come in contact with, internally or externally, as your customer. If you can channel your time and energy and focus on how you can better serve them, you will truly make a difference.

Know Your Customers

To serve your internal and external customers well, you need to not only know who they are but also what makes them happy. Knowing as much as you possibly can about your customers will make it easier for you to serve them. Find out what your customers want and then do everything in your power to get it for them. There's no greater feeling than to meet or exceed a customer's expectation. Always move in the direction of serving others. By serving others, you are serving yourself.

You also have personal customers—your family and friends. In a way, each of them has special needs that are different and unique. Parents who are service-oriented identity the needs of each child and then promote his or her personal growth.

In successful marriages, partners seek to understand and fulfill each other's needs. Good customer service means having your finger on the pulse of other people's needs and doing everything in your power to fulfill those needs.

When you wake up each morning, try to think of just one thing that you could do to make other people's lives easier as a result of your interaction with them. You show me the person with this mindset, and I'll show you someone who will be very successful.

It's the little things in life that can make a big difference. Look for the little things each day that you could do to make a positive impact on someone else. Sometimes, just acknowledging another person by saying "Hello, how you doing today?" or asking someone to join you for lunch can make a difference in that person's day. It doesn't have to be a major effort.

In the following space, list just one thing that you could do to help make someone's life at work or at home a little easier.

Just one thing to help others at work: _____

_____

_____

Just one thing to help others at home: _____

_____

_____

Now go out and make these two things happen. You will see just how easy it is to make a difference in people's lives. I guarantee that if you do these little things regularly, people will notice. There is no greater happiness than to contribute to the happiness of others.

Good Customer Service Habits

Here are some customer service habits that are good to have, regardless of who you are or what your job may be.

• *Be a good listener.* Most people who are irritated just want someone to take the time to listen to them. Often, you don't even have to solve their problem. Just listening to them goes a long way to show your customers you care about them. Try to offer suggestions that help solve the customer's problem.

• *Do what you say you will do.* This habit will help foster an environment of trust. Customers like doing business with people they trust. This means doing the things you say you will do—no excuses!

• *Deliver bad news quickly.* If you know you won't be able to deliver the product or service that you promised, for whatever reason, inform your customer immediately. No one likes to find out bad news from someone else. Don't have someone else do your dirty work for you. Stand up and be responsible.

• *Be time conscious.* In our time-oriented world, speed and reliability are vital to business success. Your time is valuable, but so is your customers' time. Try to be aware of their time constraints. Clearly understand your customers' expectations and deadlines. Then, do everything possible to meet them.

• *Go the extra mile.* This is a good way to establish rapport with your customers. Meeting a customer's expectation is good; however, exceeding a customer's expectation is great. Remember, it's often the little things that people appreciate most.

• *Offer a variety of options.* If you have to say "no" to a customer, try to offer an alternative. Let your customers decide what course of action they wish to take. Providing the customer with options helps to give the customer control over the situation.

• *Be known for integrity.* Being honest is one of the greatest virtues a person can have. The most important person you have to report to is you. Above all, respect yourself. Gandhi said, "They can not take away our self respect if we do not give it to them." Be known as an honest, respectful person.

Closing Statement

Well, there you have it—the top 10 things that I hear most people complain about most of the time. Left unchecked, complaining can turn into whining. Nobody likes being around whiners. Successful people do not whine. In fact, they seldom complain. If they do complain, they often have a solution to their problem or are in the process of finding a solution. Successful people find ways to reduce or eliminate the things people do to mess up their careers and lives.

Success doesn't happen by accident. It's not luck, being in the right place at the right time, or just performing a series of tasks effectively. Vince Lombardi said, "The spirit, the will to win, and the will to excel are the things that endure." It's not enough to want to make things happen. We must want to make things happen well-through the eyes of the customer.

If you work in an industry that has a somewhat negative reputation, you may need to work extra hard to overcome the stereotypes that people may have. Exceeding customer expectations is one way to do just that. Being consistent with quality service will help you move ahead of the competition.

Create some goals and take action. Consistently move in the direction of achieving those goals. Albert Einstein said, "The world is not dangerous because of those who do harm but because of those who look at it without doing anything." Don't be afraid to make something happen! We all have much work to do. Living by *The 10 Timeless Principles* will bring you closer to living the life you were meant to live. Good luck on your continuous journey toward success.

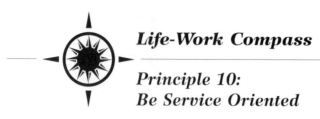

Life-Work Compass

Principle 10:
Be Service Oriented

What?

1. Create a "how may I serve you?" mentality.
2. Know who your customers are.
3. Make a positive difference in people's lives.
4. Become a good listener.
5. Exceed customer expectations.

Why?

1. To differentiate yourself from your competition at work.
2. To better serve them.
3. To contribute to the happiness of others.
4. To enhance your relationship with others.
5. To create repeat business.

How?

1. By always looking for solutions to customer problems.
2. By finding out what's important to them.
3. By doing "just one thing" to help them.
4. By not interrupting or judging others.
5. By going the extra mile.

When?

1. Anytime you interact with a customer.
2. When you talk with your customer.
3. Every day of every week.
4. When they speak.
5. Always!

About the Author

Steven R. Webber

Steve Webber is the president of Management Training Resources, Inc. (MTR), a training and consulting firm specializing in management skills training. Steve is a national speaker and consultant with over 20 years experience in a variety of fields, including Supervision, Sales, Marketing, Engineering, Customer Service, and Management Training.

Her has trained and consulted for a wide variety of companies in the service, manufacturing, healthcare, hospitality, retail, and insurance industries. Some of MTR's customers include: AC Nielsen, Chicago's Navy Pier, Cub Foods, General Electric, Harmony Health Plan, HBO Direct, Jockey, MetLife, MidAmerica Bank, Nicor Energy Services, NASA, Quill Corporation, Sears, Sherwin-Williams, United Parcel Service, Whirlpool and several major mid-western hospitals. Steve has also done work for several non-profit organizations such as Welfare-to-Work Partnership.

In addition to conducting training workshops, Steve has taught classes for the Management Center at Aurora University in Supervisory Management, Communication and Organizational Behavior. He has served as a member of the University's Advisory Board. Steve has also taught management classes at Elgin Community College and Waubonsee Community College.

Steve was a columnist for the *Kane County Chronicle*. His column was entitled *It's About Time,* and focused on providing time management techniques. He has also appeared as a guest on both local radio and cable TV.

Steve has a B.S. degree from Ball State University in Natural Resources, a second B.S. degree from Purdue University in Industrial Supervision, and a Master of Science degree in Management from Indiana Wesleyan University.

He and his wife Amy live in Naperville, Illinois, with their two children, Brian and Missy.

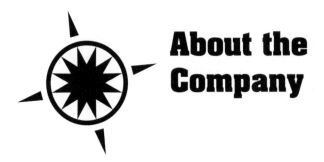

About the Company

Management Training Resources, Inc.

Steve Webber is president and owner of Management Training Resources, Inc., a training and consulting company based in Naperville, Illinois, founded in 1991.

Management Training Resources, Inc., is founded on the principles of hard work, sound values, and quality customized training. MTR has a 90 percent repeat ratio of returning customers.

We provide participants with practical tools for personal growth in a fun, interactive environment. We believe that everyone has the potential to achieve great things when given the proper resources, tools, and environment. We help people explore their full potential at work and in their personal lives.

Steve is also available for keynote speeches.

Management Training Resources:
    Toll free telephone: 1-866-687-4769
    Direct telephone: 630-717-7253
    FAX: 630-717-1513
    E-mail: Webber@mtresources.com.
    Web site: www.mtresources.com

Or, write us at:
    Management Training Resources, Inc.
    931 W. 75th Street
    Suite 137-122
    Naperville, IL 60565

Other Books by
Executive Excellence